Joseph Gargiulo is a highly successful insurance professional from New York who has prospered at his career despite having to overcome some extremely challenging obstacles in his life. With over 35 years of experience in the industry and over 5,000 clients, he currently mentors over 75 of his peers from across the country as well as military family and veterans seeking guidance as they enter the private workforce.

For my children, Joseph, Gina and Tricia, my parents,
Joe and Patricia and for all of the souls who need
a little "Joey" in their lives…

Joseph Gargiulo

BULLIED AND BLIND

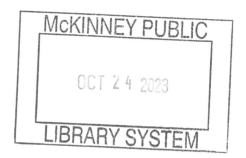

AUSTIN MACAULEY PUBLISHERS™

LONDON · CAMBRIDGE · NEW YORK · SHARJAH

Ordering Information
Quantity sales: Special discounts are available on quantity purchases by corporations, associations, and others. For details, contact the publisher at the address below.

Publisher's Cataloging-in-Publication data
Gargiulo, Joseph
Bullied and Blind

ISBN 9781638291268 (Paperback)
ISBN 9781638291275 (ePub e-book)

Library of Congress Control Number: 2023902202

www.austinmacauley.com/us

First Published 2023
Austin Macauley Publishers LLC
40 Wall Street, 33rd Floor, Suite 3302
New York, NY 10005
USA

mail-usa@austinmacauley.com
+1 (646) 5125767

Special kudos go out to my parents for supporting me through hell and back when I lost my vision and to my wife Jean who inspires me every day to keep fighting the good fight regardless of what obstacles life throws at me.

I'd like to also acknowledge the healthcare professionals who specialize in vision disorders and eye disease for your dedication and hard work towards helping those who are visually challenged.

Most importantly, I'd like to recognize anyone who has ever been bullied or who has felt like they are the runt of the litter. Just be aware that you are not alone in your fight.

Chapter 1

The other driver was unconscious as his truck raced in my direction. The weight of his limp body must have somehow caused his foot to perfectly pin the accelerator pedal to the floor. His head and torso were slumped over the wheel in a way that was so precise that it kept his vehicle on the road and continuing to accelerate, heading in my direction like a guided missile. Some people say that the runaway truck probably even managed to navigate through a few turns on that deserted road which cuts through an old, abandoned New York state psychiatric hospital in Kings Park, Long Island, where I lived at the time.

The collision was later described as a "freak accident" as well as a case of "being in the wrong place at the wrong time." I suppose those descriptions are valid because there are countless circumstances that could have delayed my trip to work that April morning in 2004.

More than likely it would have taken only a ten second deviation from my regular routine to have put me out of harm's way. But there was no miracle phone call, misplaced keys or spilled cup of coffee to delay my journey that morning and spare me the grief of what was about to happen.

Please don't make the mistake of assuming that this is another one of those ordinary sob stories that you've read countless times before. I've always been a firm believer in the concept that all things, (good or bad), happen for a reason. And as you are about to discover, (and as horrific as it may seem), my presence there on that road at exactly the worst time possible would set off what was sure to be the most meaningful chain of events in my life. As unlikely as it may seem, it was my destiny to be on that road, gliding around that blind turn in my ex-wife's brand-new Jaguar at the precise exact moment in time that his runaway truck crossed over to the wrong side of the road and into my lane.

You just embarked on an amazing journey my friend. This is a voyage that you will not soon forget, because it is going to forever change the way you live life and conquer all of its challenges.

From what I can remember, I had about a half of a second to react to the realization that there was a speeding truck on the wrong side of the road about to slam head-on into me. I've been told many times that I have very quick reflexes (especially while operating a moving vehicle). In another life I could have been a NASCAR driver, so you will have to trust me when I tell you that if there was some crazy evasive maneuver to possibly avoid that head-on collision, I would have found a way to make it happen.

It took less than an eighth of a second for my mind to evaluate the situation and determine that even in a sporty Jaguar designed to be highly maneuverable, there was simply no way to steer clear of the front of that truck on that heavily wooded road. The truck was already too close and we were both traveling too quickly. It also didn't take more than another eighth of a second for me to conclude that based upon the size of the truck and the speeds we were traveling I was going to die. Yes, I possessed enough knowledge in the sciences of physics and biology to know that the collision was going to kill me.

I always heard of the expression "when life flashes before your eyes." Until that very moment I never really appreciated exactly what those words really meant. I admit that I did not see my entire life from childhood to parenthood flash before my eyes in that remaining quarter of a second before impact, but I did immediately think of my children and my ex-wife. I remember how sad it made me feel to think that my children will have to live life without their father from that moment onward. I thought of how upsetting and unbelievable the news of my freak accident was going to sound to them and how the thought of my horrific death would haunt them for the rest of their lives.

I thought about how horrible this tragedy was going to be for the woman I was married to. The last thing any woman wants to hear is that her husband, the man who was supporting both her and her children is killed in her car less than a mile from their home as he drove to work minding his own business.

Freak accident...
In the wrong place at the wrong time...

These words might be considered acceptable descriptions of my car accident, but they certainly would not be considered to be acceptable reasons for my death for my ex-wife, children, my parents, relatives or anyone who knew and cared about me at that time. These thoughts flashed through my brain as I watched my imminent collision with that truck transpire in what felt like a slow-motion movie.

With time practically standing still it gave me the opportunity to think about all of the obstacles I managed to overcome throughout the thirty-six years of my life. My childhood social life was plagued with challenge after challenge. I always felt that if I were born a puppy, I would have been considered to be the runt of the litter, the odd-one out. I was born left-handed while most of the rest of the civilized world is not. As a child I was always physically smaller and weaker than the children my own age (and being born in late October just made it worse). I was often the first person to be picked-on by the bullies in school and one of the last ones to be picked when choosing teammates. I was a nerd. I was a geek. I was not popular and not at all considered to be "cool." Nothing comes easy when there is a target on your back and your peers despise you, especially starting at an early age.

My body not only felt weak, it was built all wrong too. Sometimes I think my body is like a bad science experiment. I've been on the operating table over a dozen times. I think the exact number of my surgeries so far is sixteen (and that is not including the dozens of medical procedures that did not require general anesthesia). I've been operated on from head to toe to repair all sorts of ailments but by far the most significant surgeries have been on my eyes. You see, by the time I was nineteen years old I lost all of the functional vision in both of my eyes due to

12

a rare eye disorder known as Keratoconus. I could still see light and colors and sometimes I could still make out large shapes but the images were so distorted that for all practical purposes I was a teenager who had become legally and functionally blind.

But thanks to modern medicine, an enormous amount of will power and three really generous eye donors I was able to overcome that blindness. Cornea transplants and some very special hard contact lenses known as 'R.G.P.s' have allowed me to manage 20/20 vision for extended periods of time throughout my life. But my newfound vision hasn't come without a price, nor has it come without a struggle.

Transplant surgery can mark the end to a significant problem like blindness or organ failure, but it can also mark the beginning of a life with new daily challenges that often go unspoken. With many corneal transplants, those new challenges are enough to discourage the most willful minds, even on a good day.

It made me incredibly sad that morning when I realized that all of the hardship that I endured over the years, (in order to stay on track with reaching the goals I've set out to accomplish in life), were a complete waste of time because I was about to die before many of those goals were reached. That sadness instantaneously turned into anger toward the driver of that vehicle for speeding directly toward me on the wrong side of the road. I also felt an incredible amount of resentment toward the universe itself for allowing me to be in that wrong place at the wrong time. Some people would question whether or not I blame God. I'm not much of a religious person, so to be honest with you during that last fraction of a second, (as I was certain that I was about to die), I never once blamed God or even asked for his forgiveness. My one and only reaction, after realizing that there was no way for me to prevent my death, was to raise one of my hands in front of my face to protect my eyes and scream out the word "NO!!!!!"

I screamed because I was so incredibly angry that this was happening to my family.

Considering the amount of grief we've endured throughout our lives compared to other families around us I would have thought that we would be given a break from the suffering for a while. But life doesn't work that way. There are no set rules when it comes to these things. The reliable scientific formulas of probability simply do not apply when trying to predict how much grief each of us will endure during our lives in comparison to our neighbors. Modern statistical analysis cannot predict the frequency of our grief. And we can all forget about the concept of equality applying to pain and suffering. As much as any of us would like to believe that we will each endure our fair share of bad luck and mental/physical anguish, the truth is that statistics are more lopsided than we care to admit. The reality is more like 10% of us on this earth are faced with enduring 90% of the real serious hardship.

Not very equal, is it?

Of course, everyone seems to think that their problems are serious. And the actual definition of "serious" when defining grief is completely subjective. But for argument's sake, if we assume that true grief is related only to health issues, you can't help but to notice that it's the same group

14

of people who are faced with serious health concerns over and over again. Walking through life as one of those runts of the litter, I can tell you that it drives us mad whenever we see a healthy person make a huge deal about a minor ailment that can be fixed in less than an hour during a regular office visit. Get your head cracked open, your eyeballs sliced and diced or your heart worked on and then talk to me about how serious your health problems are. Otherwise, be grateful that you are on the more fortunate side of the lopsided way life deals out misery.

If you or someone you know has been unfortunate enough to be among those of us who've had to contend with truly serious health problems then you can appreciate how difficult it is to work through these ordeals. You can also appreciate how upsetting it was for me that morning to know that all of that hard work and effort was about to be deemed insignificant and pointless the moment that runaway truck took it all away. My case was the extreme. I didn't just learn how to cope with the heavy punches that life threw at me, I learned how to conquer them! I became a master at converting negative energy into positive results.

The secret to my success surely was a combination of several factors. There's no doubt that all of those years of getting picked on in school and refusing to give up prepared me for the extreme challenges I would face later on in life. It's an unspoken fact that the majority of today's most powerful individuals were the nerds of the past. That is a given. Most of us who were once nerds eventually learn to live by a philosophy of unknown origin that goes something like this:

SUCCESS AND LIVING WELL IS THE
ULTIMATE REVENGE.

It's no secret that most of us nerds hold never ended grudges against those peers who used our bodies as punching bags and our self-esteems as doormats. I will be the first to admit that there is no vengeance more satisfying than to live life in ways that our bullies could only dream of living. This desire to prosper is so strong that it nurtures innovation in ways more powerful than you can ever imagine.

Self-pity was never an acceptable mindset when I was a child so there was no reason to allow it to be a way for me to cope with any problems as an adult. Instead, I became a poster boy for optimism. I took the "glass-is-half-full" outlook and made it my religion. I decided at a very young age that I would not dwell on any bad events that happened in the past. The only reason not to completely forget a bad event was so that I could avoid making a bad mistake twice. Other than that, bad memories serve no useful purpose. Bad memories have the ability to haunt us if we keep them fresh in our minds. If you hold onto too many bad memories at the same time, they will surely overwhelm your life.

Likewise, I quickly figured out that our future contains so much uncertainty that we can be driven to insanity if we allow ourselves to worry about every little detail. Don't get me wrong, I'm a huge advocate for setting goals and developing game plans to reach them. However, I am convinced that life is full of too many unpredictable variables for us to waste precious energy worrying about events that may or may not happen in the future. So the only way to live is to live it in the present. Live in the moment. Appreciate what you have. Deal with whatever you are being faced with at this point in time. This is where all of your energy should be directed.

Most important of all, even though we may have our moments where we need to complain or blow off steam, I learned that we should never, ever let anyone or anything get the best of us. This means learning to control our emotions so that we do not allow the actions of others upset us so much that they have a lasting negative effect. We should never let anything or anyone stop us in our tracks and prevent us from carrying on our lives the way we intended.

These are the principals that I developed to deal with all of the turmoil in my life. These are the ideals that molded me into the ultimate optimist, despite all of the grief and pain that life dished out at me. For many people who walk in my shoes, life is mostly about coping and learning to accept one's limitations. For most of them it's all about being grateful for what they have, instead of wasted energy focusing on the things they do not. Those were never, and will never be, acceptable terms for me to swallow. I simply refused to let any handicap or disability stand in my way of success. No matter what your situation may be, you should never let the beliefs of others define the course of your destiny.

It took a good part of my life and a great deal of pain for me to eventually evolve into the optimist I am today. Trial and error played a crucial role in that evolution. Failed attempts were what I considered to be healthy growing pains, but complete failure was never an acceptable option.

17

There is an amazing byproduct of success that's known as 'confidence.' The beautiful thing about confidence is that it also happens to be a key ingredient in the formula for sustained success. So the more successful I became, the more confidence I was able to stockpile. And the more confidence I had in my corner the more I was able to become the master of my own destiny and a jack of all trades. I gained so much confidence that there became no task or skill that I viewed to be too complicated to learn. I became one of those people who believed that if you can dream it, you can do it. I also stockpiled enough confidence to step outside of my comfort zone and accept new challenges as if I had been trained to do them.

Wrote a book that was published... done it.

Recorded underwater video of great white sharks off the coast of South Africa while diving in an anti-shark cage... done it.

Appeared on television playing at the final table of a poker tournament... done it twice.

Snorkeling over the Great Barrier reef in Australia... done it.

Stand-up comedy in front of a live audience... done it.

Played in the America versus Canada battle of the border amateur billiards tournament... done it.

Top 5% sales producer for a Fortune 100 company... done it.

Zip-lining through the rainforest in Costa Rica... done it.

Tuna and sword fishing at the Hudson Canyon/continental shelf... done it.

Climbed through the water to the top of a 180-foot waterfall in Jamaica... done it.

Handlined a 200lb shark to shore from a pier in Roatan, Honduras... done it.

Hiked the Appalachian Trail... done it.

Piloted a blimp over the city of Savannah Georgia... done it.

Sailed through the Panama Canal... done it.

Motored a Segway to the highest peak in Aruba... done it.

Swimming with dolphins... done it three times.

Helicoptered over an active volcano in Hawaii... done it.

Hiked the cliffs along the Gulf of Maine... done it.

Parasailed over the beaches of Belize... done it.

Custom-designed over two dozen ecommerce websites... done it.

Kayaking with reef sharks in the Bahamas... done it.

Lobster-diving off of Key West... done it.

As you can see, in my mind the sky is the limit to what we can do in life. Dream it and you can do it. It's really that simple. But sustained success by an extreme optimist often attracts some of the quirkiest critics. There is this entire school of thinking out there who preach that the only reason why a guy like me has such a positive attitude is because of my success. They have the formula completely lopsided, because my success did not create my positive attitude; it was my positive attitude that created my success! Little do they know that for a runt of the litter like me who has had a target on my back most of my life, confidence = power, and we all know that power = freedom. With that being said, I am living, walking proof that freedom = making dreams come true.

Another mistake my critics often make is to confuse my strong level of confidence with arrogance. Like most school-age geeks and freaks, I don't go around in my adulthood announcing to everyone I meet that I was bullied extensively throughout childhood. It's not something that we are proud to openly admit. Even my ex-wife wasn't aware of that darkness in my past. I despise arrogance because it is a trait commonly displayed by bullies. I hold my head high and walk with pride because my success is not just the product of my hard work, but because I know that it was accomplished using some very noble attributes such as 'respect,' 'ethics,' and 'charisma.' I did not cut corners or take shortcuts. I also didn't have any friends in high places to pull strings or open doors for me.

My relentless desire to succeed combined with my optimistic belief that I could are what brought me to the point that is often described with phrases such as "in the zone" and "on top of his game." Whatever words you use to describe that perfect balance that I achieved, surely you will agree how disturbing it must have felt to see that truck racing toward me about to stop me in my tracks and push me backward in more ways than one.

At the very last moment before impact I was able to catch a glimpse of the individual who was going to be responsible for ending it all. Before I died, I had to catch a glimpse of my killer. I had to know what he looked like, because it made no sense to me why that truck was being driven so rapidly toward me on the wrong side of the road.

But as odd and unlikely as this may sound, when our vehicles were close enough for me to see the person sitting there in the driver's seat, I did not see an unconscious man in his fifties. Instead I swear that what I saw was the devil himself! I know how crazy this sounds. But keep in mind that this claim is coming from someone who is indeed not much of a religious man. I swear that when I tried to look the idiot in the eyes, I found myself staring right into the darkness of hell. I found myself staring into the soul of pure evil.

I can't help but to think what an appropriate encounter it was meeting Satan within the boundaries of an abandoned psychiatric center. Surely the landscape of an institution where decades of insane minds were housed and experimented upon would be familiar grounds for Lucifer, the master of all demons. It then occurred to me that this was his playground. I had the sudden realization that this was grade school all over again, only this time I found myself face-to-face with one of the most dangerous bullies the world has ever known! I must give evil some credit here because I didn't see this one coming. It's often said that all good things must come to an end sooner or later, but I never thought I would be struck down in my prime so soon and so suddenly.

It was at that moment that I learned a secret that only I could know to be true. It became obvious to me that my car accident was not some random unlikely collision. It wasn't a case of being in the wrong place at the wrong time, just as it was not a freak accident. It was obvious that devil had an ingenious looking smirk on his face. I knew that smirk all too well from all those years of being bullied. He smirked and I'm pretty sure he even winked one of his eyes at me as he aimed that truck in my direction. He even accelerated at the last moment just to be sure that there was no way I could escape the fate that evil planned for my life. This was not an accident. It was nothing less than a well-orchestrated intentional act.

Before I could analyze the situation any further there was an incredible explosion of steel and glass as I felt a powerful shockwave begin to travel through my body. The sound was unbearable. It could have put a sonic boom to shame. The percussion was so loud and intense that my eardrums could only partially absorb it. Then there was the accompanying shockwave...Oh that shockwave! It was both painful and numbing at the same time, much like a dentist's Novocain injection, and it traveled through my bones and flesh like a violent earthquake. It reminded me of the sensation of being on a modern extreme rollercoaster ride. Only on this ride your worst fears come true. Unlike an amusement park ride that does a really great job at making you think that you are going to feel pain and intense discomfort, (even though you never actually do), this ride packs a real punch where you'd never expect it; deep inside the inner core of the body.

The first part of the deadly shockwave started in my right foot, because I somehow managed to jam that foot on the brake pedal the moment I knew there was going to be a collision. The entire front end of a modern automobile is designed to crumble like an accordion upon impact. Believe it or not, this is a safety feature. They are designed this way with the hope that as the steel crumbles it will absorb a good percentage of the shockwave. During slower, lower impact collisions this design often spares the occupants of the vehicle from having to feel the blunt force of the collision. It saves lives. It prevents many injuries. However, this safety design has limitations. The devil made sure that the speed of that truck combined with the speed of my car was more than enough to overwhelm that safety design and render it meaningless.

The truck was traveling at over seventy miles per hour...
I was driving at thirty or forty miles per hour.

The impact was like driving over a hundred miles directly into a solid stone wall.

That first shockwave traveled up my leg and through the center of my body's core where it met up with a second shockwave that started in my left hand as it firmly grasped the steering wheel. Once again, I feel the urge to make reference to an extreme rollercoaster ride, because I assimilated the sensation of coming to a sudden stop, (while wearing the Jaguar's 3-point retractable safety harness), to the way we feel while being seated within one of today's modern high-performance rollercoasters. It reminded me of how we feel on a rollercoaster when we are getting tossed around while safely locked behind the ride's safety restraints but a hundred times more powerful.

Anyone who frequents a five-star amusement park will agree that the g-forces created by instant deceleration and the stress that it puts on our body are so much different than those we feel from rapid acceleration. Rapid forward acceleration is fun and exhilarating even when it's insane like on the legendary Kingda Ka rollercoaster at Six Flags Great Adventure in New Jersey. But rapid or sudden deceleration is just plain sickening, (especially when it's unexpected). And the absolute worst extreme is when we strike a larger, faster moving object that stops us in our tracks instantly and then propels us backward while we are accelerating forward. Those are the kinds of impacts that instantly kill us.

"Blunt force trauma."

Until that moment I never realized exactly what those words meant. Coroners, police and medical examiners often use those words to summarize the destructive effects of the shockwave created when two vehicles moving rapidly in opposite directions collide.

In my situation the two intense shockwaves united into a single massive shockwave somewhere in the center of my body, near my vital organs. Those who study physics could explain in great detail how the energy travels through the body the way small waves ripple across the surface of a pond after a rock is thrown into the water. Physicists can also give the scientific reason why the energy continues to circulate throughout the body because it has no place else to go.

My experience confirmed their hypothesis as all of the energy travelled up my neck and into my head, where it indeed found no way to escape. I felt my brain bouncing around inside my skull as the shockwave swirled around like an F-5 tornado inside my head. I tried desperately to grip on to life as each rotation of that shockwave around my skull tore apart pieces of my mind. And with each tear I lost random blocks of memory, logic, and brain function. I focused upon the vision of my ex-wife and children and held on with all of my will. I held on for what felt like an eternity as all that destructive energy kept on spinning inside my head with no place to escape.

Then all was silent and everything went black…

Chapter 2

Some of my best memories as a child revolve around the ocean. Summertime consisted of going to the beach with my mom on the weekdays and fishing with my dad out on the boat on the weekends. One of the benefits of living on an Island that's 118 miles long is the vast amount of coastline. When you factor in the shoreline of the north and south, forks on the east end, as well as the coasts of all of the barrier islands, peninsulas, bays, harbors, creeks and canals, there is easily around a thousand miles of shoreline here. This translates into endless saltwater recreational opportunities.

When you live on an island you eventually discover the odd fact that the majority of an island's population rarely takes advantage of the shoreline opportunities. This is true, even when the water is always less than a fifteen-minute drive away. Even more peculiar is that a good amount of the residents on an island actually despise the water. I've found this to be true even in the state of Hawaii where everyone is an islander.

So even though we live on the most populated island in the United States, we can still find peace and tranquility by escaping to the water. My parents were the first to teach me this secret. The Atlantic Ocean and the shoreline were like a second home to me. Over the years I became skilled in recreational fishing, clamming and crabbing and I learned to appreciate the practice of taking only what we planned to eat and returning everything else to the sea. My father saw to it that like him, I became addicted to every sort of angling opportunity that the sea had to offer, from the delicate and tranquil art of fly fishing, (using ultra-light tackle all the way), to the intense fast-paced arena of big game offshore, and everything in-between.

I had so much fun out on the water that it didn't dawn on me that perhaps my dad had an alternative motive for taking me out there. Of course, I'm sure it was rewarding as a father to teach his son the ways of the sea and how to perfect each of those angling skills. And I'm sure that he knew that so much of that knowledge also applies toward more serious areas of life, including the business world.

It probably should have come as no surprise to me that I chose a profession in sales and marketing, because there are countless similarities between angling and marketing. The concepts required to put together a successful catch on the water happens to also work incredibly well in the business world, when utilized by a sales force. I know for a fact that I love my sales job so much, because I get the same rush and satisfaction every day I'm out there selling, as I do on a new fishing trip.

All those reasons to get me off of land and out of the water were surely true, but I also think that on some level my dad knew that I needed the escape. I'm sure he was aware that I was a sort of a social misfit, who had trouble fitting in with my peers.

You see, unlike most of the kids in my neighborhood on the south shore of the Island, I was not a native Long Islander. I was originally born in Brooklyn and did not move to Long Island until I was in grade school. Just like most new kids who move to an established neighborhood, I found it incredibly difficult to fit in. I was a scrawny, nerdy-looking kid with a foreign accent, who wore strange clothing. I knew how to play street games like stoopball, stickball, and red-light/green-light very well, but I couldn't find anyone else who knew the rules or was interested in playing. Everyone seemed to be more preoccupied with sports like football, soccer and little league baseball, as well as a strange looking American Indian sport they called lacrosse.

I also didn't have any older brothers or sisters to pave the way for a meaningful social life. Being the oldest of four children, it was left to me to be the pioneer of this new territory. I did make a new friend or two here and there, but for the most part, I found it bitterly frustrating how unwelcoming the other kids made a newcomer feel.

As nasty as it sounds, the children in my new town made it a pastime to torture those who were new to the neighborhood. The bigger problem was that there appeared to be no amount of time that could pass before new kids were no longer regarded as 'new.' It was like having a target permanently tattooed on my back for the entire duration of grade school.

This sort of foolish behavior was in deep contrast with how I was taught to treat people and to what I was accustomed to in my old neighborhood in Brooklyn.

The statement, 'we moved from Brooklyn to Long Island,' can only make sense to true New Yorkers. To anyone else unfamiliar with the area who simply picks up and examines a map, the concept of moving from Brooklyn to Long Island will make as little sense as me saying that we moved from New York to the United States. That's because technically speaking, Brooklyn is actually part of Long Island. It's a very populated area that's situated on the westernmost portion of the island. There is no need to cross a bridge or travel through a tunnel to go from my old neighborhood in Brooklyn to my new one on Long Island, because there is no body of water separating Brooklyn from the rest of Long Island.

Geographically speaking, Brooklyn is on Long Island. But in terms of appearance, culture, economy and a dozen other factors, the neighborhoods might as well be situated on different continents with thousands of miles of ocean separating the two. Brooklyn is Brooklyn. Long Island is Long Island. In-between the two is the often-forgotten borough of Queens, which acts almost like an invisible force field preventing the contrasting characteristics of the neighborhoods from ever blending together.

Speaking of Brooklyn neighborhoods, most people aren't aware that even though Brooklyn is a borough of New York City, it's still divided into dozens of distinct neighborhoods that are like mini cities themselves. There are actually more than six dozen distinct neighborhoods. My family comes from the area known as Bensonhurst. It was prominently an Italian neighborhood, back when I lived there in the late 1960s to mid-1970s. We lived off of

18th Avenue, which was the neighborhood's main thoroughfare.

18th Avenue consisted of hundreds of small Italian family-owned businesses that had been handed down from one generation to the next. Imagine the world's best shopping mall with the ultimate selection of shopping, food and services, but instead of being housed inside of one large building, the shops lined both sides of a busy city street. That's the best way to describe 18th Avenue. Just as we have the world at our fingertips today via the internet, back then you could obtain anything you needed by simply walking down 18th Avenue.

There have always been a number of different ways to classify the different Brooklyn neighborhoods. I suppose the most obvious used to be in terms of ethnicity. For instance, neighborhoods such as Bay Ridge, Dyker Heights, and Bath Beach, (like Bensonhurst), were primarily Italian-American, while neighborhoods such as Borough Park, Midwood and Crown Heights, were primarily Jewish. This may seem to have been the most obvious way to classify the neighborhoods, but for the millions of us who actually lived in Brooklyn in the 60s and 70s it was not as important as knowing which neighborhoods were safe and which were not.

Instead of labeling neighborhoods by the cultures and religions of the people who lived there, we were more concerned about labeling them with two words: 'Good' or 'Bad.' A 'good' neighborhood was one where you could walk down the street at night and stand a good chance of not having your wallet stolen. A 'bad' neighborhood was one where you could not park your car while you ran into a store for ten minutes, unless you wanted your hubcaps and car stereo stolen. Using these real-world criteria, it was understood that there were also some bad Italian neighborhoods, just as there were some bad neighborhoods where other ethnic groups lived. But in terms of good or bad, Bensonhurst ranked among the very safest during that time period. And for a young Italian boy, one of the neighborhood's own offspring, it was safer than living in the White House.

I remember being no more than four years old, riding my bicycle with training wheels down 70th Street, where we lived in a small apartment above my maternal grandparents' home. When I reached the corner at 19th Avenue, I turned without hesitation toward 71st Street, because I knew I had permission to ride my bike anywhere around our city block, (as long as I stayed on the sidewalk and never crossed or entered a street). There was no concern about pedophiles, just as it was unheard of for a child to be abducted. So, without a worry in the world I would pedal that bike all alone around the corner and further away from my home.

I still recall the excitement of making the next turn in my journey toward 18th Avenue. I always stopped to look across the street to the corner house on the other side of 71st Street and 18th Avenue where my dad grew up and his parents still lived. It was always fun waving to one or both of those grandparents as I pedaled on toward 18th Avenue, (which was always the highlight of the trip).

Once anyone made that turn from the tranquil residential street on to the hustle and bustle of the Avenue, it was like travelling into another dimension. Hearing countless conversations in native Sicilian dialect, combined with the mixed aromas of grilled pork sausage and baked semolina bread, as well the sight of all of sorts of hand-woven exotic fabrics in an amazing range of colors, was enough to convince anyone who turned that corner that they were now somewhere along the tropical coast of the Mediterranean Sea.

As a four-year-old I had my favorite shops where most four-year-olds would love to stop on that strip of 18th avenue from 71st Street back to 70th Street. I was particularly intrigued by the shops that afforded me a look-see at something alive and exotic. The fish market was an awesome place to stop for a few minutes, if you could bear the awful smell. There was usually a bucket outside the market where I could catch a glimpse of spiny sea urchins as they walked along on their hundreds of legs. Out on the sidewalk the fish market usually also displayed a tank full of live snails in shells bearing very interesting markings. Naturally these exotic offerings were being sold by the market as food, but every so often the man in the doorway would allow me to hold and play with one or more of those peculiar little critters as if they were my pets.

Speaking of pets, a few doors down from that market was a tiny gift store where the owner often stocked one of the most popular pets of that era. They weren't a breed of dog or cat, (as you would likely expect), because as much as each of them do make excellent pets, they also require a great deal of attention. They also can prove to be quite costly, between the cost of their food and veterinarian fees. No, the most popular pet of that time was much less expensive and super low maintenance. You might never guess it unless you lived through the early 1970s as a child, and even if you did, you may not recall that the most popular pet back then was none other than the tiny baby turtle!

At no more than an inch or two in length, they were the cutest little critters a child, like me, ever saw. I had one of my own back at the apartment, but I still loved stopping by the store and watching other children pick out their new pet turtles. The owner had a giant tank full of several species. I vaguely recall the most popular having a greenish colored shell and really cool looking red or yellow stripes along the sides of their faces. Once a child chose one of the turtles, the store owner would set them up with a small fish bowl containing a tiny habitat consisting of some small pieces of slate and a plastic palm tree.

The baby turtle fad turned into one of the biggest crazes of the 1970s. But there were some problems that everyone failed to consider. For starters, baby turtles don't remain babies forever. Eventually they will outgrow even large fish bowls; that's if they didn't die from the toxicity of living in their own feces first. Those fish bowls didn't have any sort of filtration system. I remember the only way to keep the water from turning brown and obnoxious smelling was to empty the bowl and clean it three or four times a day. So much for the idea of a low maintenance pet! And there weren't many children, (including myself), who really had the time and the energy to clean their turtle's fish bowl over and over again.

To make matters even worse, shortly after the baby turtle craze took off, so did a new and unusually large outbreak of salmonella poisoning in young children. Salmonella is one of those bacteria that can easily pass between animals and humans. It didn't take very long for some really smart scientists to discover that the baby turtles and their dirty smelling fish bowls were a perfect breeding ground for the salmonella bacteria. Children across the country were coming down with high fevers and severe diarrhea, and their pet turtles were to blame. Sometime around 1975 the Food and Drug Association had to step in and put an end to it all by banning the sale of turtles shorter than four inches in length to prevent further spread of the dangerous infection.

With the news that our pet turtles were infested with salmonella, it provided a much-needed explanation why all of the children in the neighborhood appeared to have contracted food poisoning. People only notice when a child gets sick. It takes a widespread epidemic for someone to casually notice that a child did not. And the fact that I was never infected by that salmonella epidemic, (while all of the other children in the neighborhood did), sparked only a mild level of curiosity. It was easy to conclude that it was pure luck as to why I was spared the agony. Not one person, (including my physician), would have ever guessed that this was actually the first obvious clue that there was something remarkably different about my immune system.

Nobody ever had a reason to take notice to the fact that it had become a regular occurrence for my immune system to ward off infections that would have normally been a nuisance for a typical child's body. Variation in the way an immune system functions is more of a factor for a person if their immune system fails to perform as strong as it should, and not the other way around. However, it can cause some serious havoc for a person if they ever need to become a transplant recipient. But as a young child, there was still no indication that anything was even remotely wrong with my eyesight, so the clue that my body possessed the unusual ability to successfully defeat potent microbes, (better than the immune systems of all of the other children my age), was forgotten as quickly as the pet baby turtle craze.

Back on 18th Avenue, the only thing for a child that was better than viewing the live critters, was sampling the food. Lucky for us there was no shortage of free samples being offered to children. It's no secret that gourmet cuisine is the backbone of our Italian culture. Every event in our lives, from the celebration of birth to the mourning of death revolves around preparing, serving and eating our favorite foods. Needless to say, the food being sold on 18th Avenue was absolutely out of this world. It was not uncommon to meet people who travelled great distances to our neighborhood to purchase the fresh cannoli, artisan baked bread, aromatic pizza pies and fresh mozzarella cheese.

In the summertime, my personal favorite was the homemade chocolate Italian ice that was sold through the walk-up window of the bakery on the corner of 18th Avenue and 70th Street. People who take great pride in knowing that the food will bring joy to all who consume it, prepare the best tasting food. This is true whether the person is preparing a complex entrée, or something as simple as frozen flavored water. It always tastes better when it's made with love. One lick of any of those flavored Italian ices from that bakery was all it took to know that somebody indeed took great pride in making them.

You see, 'pride' was the hallmark of the neighborhood. Being immigrants, (or first- generation Americans whose families came over here from Italy mostly during the Great Depression), none of the families in the neighborhood had very much money. But what they did have was an enormous work ethic. As a result, most of them families owned decent homes where they lived relatively comfortable lives. It was a place where undertakers and janitors were as respectable trades as doctors and firemen, because it was understood that the world could not function smoothly without competent people filling each of those roles. When each person's exact profession was taken out of the equation, it allowed everyone to be judged based upon what mattered the most; how much he or she 'cared' about the quality of their work.

It's quite obvious to me now that spending those early years of my life growing up in an environment where I was surrounded by people who loved to produce excellence had a major impact on my own desire to excel and succeed. It inspired me to always strive to live up to my potential. It also taught me not to cut corners or take unnecessary shortcuts, because doing so would just cheat me out of the satisfaction of completing a difficult task done correctly. I learned that there is something more rewarding than money that can be earned from a job well done. And most importantly of all, I learned to respect all occupations equally, because they are all just as important to society and the world's economy.

Unfortunately, any mention of pride in a positive manner will immediately spark some major opposition from many people who worship the bible, because pride is regarded as one of the seven deadly sins. As a matter of fact, pride is regarded as the sin of all sins. The argument is that pride is a horrible sin, because it is a preoccupation with self, instead of with God. That's completely understandable if a person's motive is nothing other than to excel at others expense, or for the bragging rights of being better than everyone else. It's taught that this very behavior is the root of all evil, because it is what transformed Lucifer into Satan and condemned him to hell. It is also what drove Eve to pick the forbidden fruit in the Garden of Eden. But common human wisdom dictates that pride doesn't always have to be about selfishness or taking credit away from God for his work, nor does it have to always be about arrogance. Despite what religion teaches, most proud people are not on some sort of quest to attempt to be better than God, or take his place.

As a runt of the litter, (who was the unfortunate recipient of some very mean acts), I know from first-hand experience that there actually happens to be a very large disconnect between pride and evil. Some of the worst bullies I ever encountered depended upon their evil behavior to compensate for their extremely low levels of pride and self-esteem. Likewise, people like me, who were bullied extensively, would have never survived many of those ordeals had it not been for our pride.

The truth is that pride usually makes the world a better place to live, because it motivates people to help others and to do the right thing. It also motivates working people to produce the highest quality products that they are capable of. There is no sin in giving someone the best haircut that you can and being glad to do so, just as there is no sin in repairing someone's sink with so much confidence that you can guarantee that it will never break again.

The concept of pride, as was demonstrated to me by everyone I knew, was the root of all good and not the sin of all sins. The pride taught to me was a virtue, not something that had anything to do with being conceited or self-centered. There are countless good, proud people in the world, just as there are many humble evil people. I get the whole reason why religion dictates that pride is a sin. It's just so incredibly obvious that the pride that I'm familiar with doesn't even vaguely resemble the pride that the Old Testament warns us about.

My ability to sort out and make sense of these kinds of dilemmas that life throws at us is yet another treasure that I must credit back to the old neighborhood. Most of the men in the neighborhood were tradesman and most of the women were proud homemakers. The vast majority of the people I called relatives and neighbors never stepped foot in a college or university. A good percentage of them didn't even graduate from high school. Naïve outsiders often make the mistake of stereotyping the people from the old neighborhood as being simple-minded and uneducated. Truth be told, and as strange as this may sound, in all of my life I have never been surrounded by so many intelligent people as I did back when I lived in Brooklyn.

It is a well-known fact among the people from the old neighborhood that the term 'street smart' originated in Brooklyn as a way to describe the vast knowledge that the residents possessed about life. In contrast to 'book smarts,' (that anyone could learn on their own at a library), street smarts was the name to describe how this wisdom could only be learned through real-life experiences, or from spending time around people who were willing to pass on this knowledge.

Being street smart is more complex than what most people would imagine. It's more than being a master at using good common sense or making sound decisions. It also happens to be about knowing how to relate to people from all walks of life, as well as having a keen sense of awareness of one's surroundings. To be truly "street smart" means to be wise to the ways of the world and to the behavior of the people who live in it.

The elders of my childhood may not have been well-versed in many of the works of William Shakespeare or in any of the theories of Albert Einstein. However, their logic and problem-solving methodology, (along with their fascinating negotiating tactics), are examples of the outside-of-the-box kind of skills that were drilled into my head by my elders. It wasn't until later in life, when I was in high school, (and then again as I went on to be the first person on either side of my family to graduate college), that I realized that I had been empowered with some remarkable intellectual gifts that are rarely, if ever, taught in books or in the traditional classroom structure.

Another common mistake that people from outside of the neighborhood made was to assume that we were out of touch with nature, because we lived in a hectic city. What they failed to realize was that almost every family had a home or a place to visit outside of the city where they could unwind from the chaos.

Our family had a house my grandfather built for us on a beautiful piece of wooded property that he and my grandmother purchased on the side of a mountain, high up in the Catskill Mountain range. This was our paradise. This was where we would get in tune with nature.

Escaping to the house that grandpa built was our opportunity to pause and experience the simplicity of country living.

There is no shortage of valuable lessons to be learned while living and playing in the mountains. You quickly discover that many aspects of life take on new meanings when you take away the challenges and confusion of living in a city among millions of other people. It's obvious that you can breathe easier with the crisp, fresh mountain air. A little less obvious is the fact that your mind can function more smoothly in the country, where it can find a little extra time to analyze and process information, as well as tap into its creative abilities. Some of the all-time greatest masterpieces, (in terms of works of art, as well as literature), can be credited to great minds that swapped noisy and polluted city settings for pristine countryside sanctuaries to maximize their creative energy.

Vacationing in the country also afforded me the opportunity to learn skills that were otherwise prohibited in the city or on Long Island. At a very young age I learned how to properly use a firearm, as well as how to ride a motorcycle. I learned how to chop firewood with an axe and how to fish, hunt and navigate in the rough terrain. I learned everything I could about the plants, animals and aquatic life that inhabited the countryside. As time went on, I became quite the outdoorsman and I loved every minute of it. Staying true to the 'keep only what you plan to eat' ideology, I learned to respect the countryside, just as much as my father taught me to respect the sea.

When you spend enough time in the outdoors, whether in the mountains or on the water, you learn to respect Mother Nature and the massive powers she possesses. This is especially true when it comes to developing an appreciation for changes in the weather. Intense storm systems can materialize rather quickly on the open water, as well as in the mountains. High winds, strong lightning and low visibility are examples of some of the mariner's and outdoorsman's worst nightmares. I was taught how one of the key street-smart abilities, (having a keen sense of awareness of one's surroundings), was even more important in the wild than it was on the streets.

Awareness is also a survival skill in the outdoors. Up high in the mountains it includes such things as being able to identify and avoid poisonous plants, dangerous animals and hazardous terrain. Out on the water it includes being able to identify and steer clear of hazardous shoals or floating debris. In both places, awareness meant learning how to be able to sense subtle changes in the weather that might be the first early warning signs that stormy weather was just beyond the horizon.

Back on the streets of Brooklyn, awareness was all about anticipating the actions of the people around you. Cities are havens for criminals. The most dangerous criminals are often the most intelligent criminals. By far, the best protection from the evil city masterminds has been to use keen awareness to stay one step ahead of them. This reminds me of the day that my dad made the unpopular decision to move our family from the busy streets of Brooklyn to the greener pastures of Long Island.

I was scheduled for my first ever eye examination at an ophthalmologist. We walked up to 18th Avenue and headed toward the corner of 69th Street, where my dad last parked his car. But we soon discovered that his car had been stolen. It became obvious to him at that moment that the old neighborhood was beginning to change. Right then and there his decision to move was made. It was unpopular at the time, because it was unheard of to put any sort of distance between the relatives. Practically everyone we were related to in the United States lived within a two-mile radius. It also didn't help that my father's assumption that the neighborhood was about to change seemed so obscure at the time to everyone else.

In less than a year we moved to our new home on Long Island, about an hour's drive away. A few years later some of my aunts and uncles started to notice that the neighborhood had indeed started to change. And, just as my father had anticipated, the grandparents eventually decided to relocate too. Many Brooklyn families relocated because of the undesirable changes. But what all of us failed to realize was that it was the world itself that was changing, (not just the neighborhood). It just felt like the changes were unique to us in Brooklyn, because they were more pronounced and showed face there first. This was due to the modern fast-paced New York lifestyle.

Most worldly changes take place in the city long before the rest of the world. This is true for art, music fashion, food and most aspects of society. It's also true for transformations in society itself. Most changes, (good or bad), happen in the city first. Unknown to any of us at the time, the world was losing much of the last of its innocence. An era was soon to come when it would no longer be safe to leave our doors unlocked or for children to wander the streets alone. It would prove to be a time when it would no longer be possible to easily distinguish between good neighborhoods and bad ones. In that new era there would be no limit to where, when or how evil would strike.

New acts of crime that were previously uncommon in Bensonhurst, (like my father's stolen car), were merely small glimpses of what was coming. Sadly, many people confused the deterioration of the neighborhood with new changes in its ethnic composition. It's no secret that Brooklyn is a magnet for immigrants. When houses all over Brooklyn were put up for sale by the immigrants of yesteryear and their descendants, a new wave of immigrants was more than happy to purchase those homes and take their place. It was convenient at the time to blame the spike in crime on the arrival of those new ethnic groups. But truth-be-told, everyone who lived in the old neighborhood was well aware that the changes arrived long before any of those newcomers ever stepped foot in this country.

When the Italian families began to move away, many of them sold their small 18th Avenue businesses too. Being savvy opportunists themselves, the new immigrants scooped up those storefronts the moment they were put on the market. Times were changing. The old neighborhood as we knew it was evolving, because the world itself was evolving. And my father had the foresight to see it all coming early on.

By the way, ironically or symbolically, I never made it to the eye doctor in Brooklyn that day, and for whatever reason the appointment was never rescheduled.

I guess on some level I could probably hold some sort of grudge against the hoodlums who stole my father's car. Part of me believes that it wouldn't be far-fetched at all to blame them for my lack of eye care as a young child as well. Then again, I, (of all people), should know better that this is how the world works. Street smarts dictate how we should take the necessary precautions to avoid getting caught off-guard by those unusual, (and often unexpected), twists and turns in the road of life.

I stayed true to this thinking even when I woke up in the aftermath of that nasty car accident uncertain as to whether or not I was experiencing some sort of ghostly afterlife moment, or if I had managed to beat the odds and miraculously survive. Trust me, that was no easy task, because there is nothing worse than not knowing if you are dead or alive.

Chapter 3

I never figured out how long I was unconscious after the collision with the truck in 2004.

It may have been only a few minutes, or it could have been much longer. Coming out of unconsciousness was a familiar experience for me. It felt exactly like waking up from general anesthesia. I had the usual difficulty focusing my vision, my mind was in a fog and my mouth was dry like cotton. As in the case with many of my post-operative recoveries from induced unconsciousness, I had an odd taste on my tongue and lips. Only this time, it was the taste of some sort of burnt powder, rather than the foul taste of anesthesia gas, but I was still way too groggy to figure out why.

I tried to rapidly blink my eyes to clear my eyesight, but it quickly became apparent to me that my eyes were functioning properly. I just needed my brain to remember how to operate them. I knew that I was still sitting in the driver's seat, but not much of the chaos I was seeing around me was making any sense. It looked sort of like the aftermath of a war zone. I felt like I was sitting in the middle of a maze of torn wires, mangled plastic and crushed metal.

Now that I think about it, it was a small miracle that I could see anything at all out of my eyes. I say this, because somehow both of my special R.G.P. contact lenses remained intact and in place, floating in the center of my corneas where they belonged.

R.G.P. stands for 'rigid gas permeable.' It's a fancy phrase to describe a modern type of hard contact lens that is porous to allow oxygen to penetrate through to the surface of the cornea. They are a critical component in the way cornea transplants allow those of us with the Keratoconus disease to gain back our vision. Cornea transplant surgeries rarely, (if ever), restore vision back to 20/20 on their own. The delicate microsurgery merely allows us to have the ability to wear contact lenses to obtain clear vision.

R.G.P.s are the contact lenses of choice to perform this duty because of the way they hold their shape. It's the R.G.P.s that allow us to once again obtain 20/20 vision. When you hear about how many different times and stupid funny ways I've lost one or both of these tiny $300/pair lenses, you'll appreciate how crazy it is that both lenses remained in my eyes after that head-on collision.

When the gears in my brain finally started to move enough to produce my first rational thought, my survivor instincts immediately took over. The image of my cell phone and the numbers 9-1-1 appeared out of the fog in my head. My memory was cohesive enough to recall that I normally place my cell phone on the passenger seat whenever I drive alone in a car. I also managed to understand that anything in the car that wasn't bolted down or secured in place would have been launched forward like a projectile. This meant that the most likely place to locate my cell phone was on the car mat in front of the passenger seat.

That's when I felt my first serious jolt of pain. I didn't realize that I must have forgotten to unbuckle my seatbelt. When I leaned over, I instantly felt a cramp-like pain across my chest where the seatbelt shoulder strap made contact with my body. Unbeknownst to me at the time, the sudden forward force of my body against the seatbelt harness during the collision caused an injury that would later be easily identifiable by the telltale bruising across my chest and abdomen. I would later learn that this is a common injury for survivors of high-impact automobile accidents. The bruising is referred to in the medical field as the SBM or Seat Belt Mark sign. The scary part is that it's often associated with a high rate of significant organ injuries.

Lucky me, right?

When the pain dissipated enough for me to move again, I was able to unlock the seatbelt easier than I had expected. Being in the auto insurance business, I often hear horrible stories about how seatbelt locks malfunction all the time, even after minor collisions. This is such a   common occurrence that fireman and police officers carry a special seatbelt cutter tool as part of their standard equipment.

After releasing my body from the lifesaving grip of my seatbelt, I was able to reach over and feel my way around for my cell phone. After a few seconds I grabbed on to something made out of plastic that felt strangely familiar. I brought the object closer to my face and held it up for   a better view. At first, I was dumbfound. It was a curved dark piece of plastic that fit comfortably   in my grip as if it was meant to be there, yet I didn't have a clue what the heck it was. I must have looked like such an idiot sitting there examining this object for several minutes like a chimpanzee examining a flashlight for the first time. Finally I realized why the item felt so   familiar and comfortable in my grip, it was the handle to my coffee mug!

A few minutes later, my brain finally flipped on all of the switches to bring my vision to full operating capacity and into normal focus. It was at that moment that I realized the area where I was sitting was like the crash cage of a racecar after one of those high-speed collisions, (that practically destroys the car, except for the reinforced protective cage around the car's cockpit). I realized that the entire car around me was crushed like an accordion, and everything inside the car was practically disintegrated, including myself.

That handle I had found moments earlier was all that was left of my coffee mug; the rest of it was shattered into hundreds of pieces. The coffee itself was plastered all over the car's   mangled dashboard and windshield. I became aware of the stench of cold coffee that consumed this small cavity that was once a roomy luxury car's interior. At the time, I wish I could have had just one mouthful of coffee, or any liquid to help with my dry mouth, and to wash away that awful mysterious burnt powder taste.

Every time I come out of anesthesia, I find it incredibly difficult to stay awake and focus. My mind drifts in and out of consciousness. This was no different. Even with a normal night of sleep in me, I still had the demeanor of someone with severe sleep apnea. At one point I drifted into a sleep that was so deep that I was actually awakened by the sound of my own snoring! I then gasped for air through my mouth like I had been suffocating, because my nostrils were almost completely clogged from inhaling so much of that still mysterious burnt powder, that was floating in the air around me.

I needed help. The lack of movement from inside of what remained of the truck suggested to me that anyone in that truck, who managed to survive, probably wasn't going to provide much assistance. Having earned the prestigious rank of Eagle Scout in the *Boy Scouts of America* when I was a teenager, I must have spent a hundred hours of learning first aid skills over the years. I knew all too well that step one of any first aid technique is to call for professional help. Thanks to my training, the numbers 9-1-1 once again became my focus, so I, once again, resumed the search for my cell phone. I finally was able to retrieve it from the rubble, but before I could dial those three crucial lifesaving numbers and press the 'send' button on the keypad, the memory banks inside my head somehow managed to remind my consciousness that the collision took place in an area with absolutely ZERO cell phone signals.

There isn't very much reputable scientific evidence out there that can prove that cell phone towers are hazardous to our health, yet somehow a group of influential people with too much time on their hands managed to convince my town to block the construction of a much-needed cell tower in my neighborhood. I have to tell you that the only thing worse that morning than being convinced that I was about to die in a head-on collision with a runaway truck, was the thought that I may have survived the impact, but still would

49

die because I couldn't call for help. The error message 'call failed' on my phone that moment confirmed that my worst fear was indeed my reality.

There is no scientific evidence needed to comprehend that a lack of immediate medical assistance for someone severely injured will most likely be hazardous to that person's health. That's a real threat that needs to be addressed; yet it gets neglected on a daily basis, because somehow the paranoid idiots get their way without an ounce of scientific evidence to support their delusional ideas that cell phone towers are dangerous. I wish one of them were injured with me inside of that wreckage that day, and then see if they still think that it's okay that my neighborhood has no cell phone signal.

As an extremely passionate person myself, I appreciate their desire to keep the world safe for all of us. I just wish they would have performed some research on the topic before using their influential powers to ban cell towers that could be saving lives. It's so obvious that they didn't do their homework first because if they had any knowledge whatsoever about the technology, they would know that cell phones are TWO-WAY radio devices that have to transmit a signal back to the tower in order to work. The slightest research on the subject would have taught them how they should be more worried about the radio waves that their cell phones emit, since they use them so close to their brains and bodies. They would have also learned that the radio frequencies that cellular towers transmit are much more intermittent and far weaker than those we receive on a daily basis from our local radio and television stations.

Of course, this is one of those debates that will go on endlessly across the country. As long as cell phone technology exists, so will the paranoia about the towers. And unless government officials are willing to play hardball, there will always be cellular dead zones.

Speaking about dead zones, that day did make me realize that the term, 'dead zone,' was ironically a very appropriate choice of words to describe these places, where despite amazing advances in modern communication technology, we can still die from not being able to perform that basic first aid step number one – call for professional help. With no way to call for help my attention quickly turned toward the sight of what appeared to be small puffs of smoke rising from the crushed hood of the truck.

For the very first time that morning my heart began to race as I realized that the source of the smoke was a liquid that was dripping on a hot surface. The liquid was most likely antifreeze, or some other nonflammable liquid, like windshield wiper fluid. But the distinct aroma of gasoline fumes in the air, hinted that there was a real possibility that I had just seconds to escape, before being engulfed in an inferno.

This circumstance presented me with the mother of all dilemmas. My street-smart instincts told me to get the hell out of there, if I could. But my first aid training told me that it was incredibly risky to do anything other than sit there and wait for help. Leaving my seat would break the golden first-aid rule of minimizing movement of anyone involved in a major accident, because of the fear that the person may have sustained an injury to the spine. If my spine was injured, there was a very good chance that I could have

51

crippled myself. One wrong move of my neck could have paralyzed my entire body. That's why you see paramedics always use a neck brace on accident victims whenever there is the slightest chance of an injury to the neck or spine.

Convinced that help wasn't heading my way any time soon, and faced with an overwhelming amount of evidence that remaining stationary in my seat would put my life in jeopardy, it became obvious that the only logical thing to do, was to get the hell out of the wreckage while I still could. So, without another thought, I reached for the car door handle with my left hand and attempted to open the door.

That was a big mistake. I felt a jolt of horrible pain throughout my hand when I attempted to use it to grip the door handle. Unlike the wide-spread pain that I felt across my chest, this pain was a sharp, stabbing sensation. I was certain that most of the knuckles and bones were shattered into tiny sharp pieces, as if a sledgehammer had smashed my hand. To my surprise though, X-rays and magnetic resonance imaging would later help radiologists determine that all 27 bones in that hand were completely intact. The scans revealed that my bones were badly bruised, but not fractured. They also showed evidence that the ligaments in my wrist were badly sprained due to possibly being hyper-extended backward.

Despite what the radiology reports would eventually say, the pain I felt when attempting to use my hand was unbearable enough to convince me at the time that my hand was broken and useless. It felt like I had hundreds of tiny needles under the surface of my skin. It's a well-known fact that sprains usually hurt much more than broken bones. Anyone who has had the opportunity to compare a simple fracture with a serious sprain will surely agree. As a matter of fact, hospital emergency rooms across the country are crowded with patients who mistaken sprained ligaments for broken bones, based upon the severe level of pain. It's a common mistake, because sprains hurt like a son of a bitch. Combine a severe sprain with bruising and you have the perfect recipe for an injury that'll stop most people in their tracks.

So with my dominant left hand as useless to me at that moment as a pile of Jell-O, I reached across my body with my right hand, and in one swift motion, I somehow managed to open the door. I was then able to pry it away from the car enough to slip my body out. That's when I first discovered that there was something seriously wrong with my right foot and leg. When I tried to walk, I fell to the pavement because they couldn't support my weight. It felt like they were no longer attached to my body.

I usually have an incredibly strong stomach, but that horrible sensation, combined with the extreme pain, made me incredible nauseous. It was a very odd experience knowing that the internal mechanical parts inside my ankle and knee were no longer securely connected and functioning. It's one of those surprises that will always manage to catch a person off-guard.

When we stand up, we take for granted that all of the internal components will be securely attached to each other, just as they had been since the day we were born.

I would later learn that the energy from the shockwave was so strong, that it caused an instant explosion inside of my foot. There are 107 ligaments in the human foot. In a split second   that shockwave ripped most of them off the bones where they had been securely attached.

Ligaments connect bones to other bones. They provide stability for our joints. Some of them   serve the purpose of limiting, or even preventing certain movement. There are 26 bones and 33   joints in the human foot. My foot was rendered almost useless without ligaments to hold it all together. The term 'Loosey-Goosey' was chosen by my podiatrist to be the most appropriate term   to describe the instability in my foot.

If that wasn't bad enough, as the force continued up my leg, it actually caused my knee to   bend and hyperextend completely in the wrong direction. When my knee folded up and   backward upon itself, the motion tore my anterior cruciate ligament, (better known as the ACL).   The ACL is a ligament that is critical to knee stability. In addition to preventing the joint from   rotating in ways that it was never designed to rotate, the ACL is the only thing preventing the tibia from sliding out in front of the femur.

I suspect that the obnoxious sensation that caused the right side of my body to crumble to the ground that morning was indeed the feeling of the lower part of my leg sliding in front of and   out of line with the top part of my leg. If the pain and instability in my foot wasn't enough to   cause me to collapse and fall to the pavement, the injury to my knee surely was. And the two   injuries combined were downright crippling!

As startling as it was to discover that I was too injured to walk on my own, my journey to   the pavement was more shocking when I heard a woman scream as I fell to the asphalt. I was   able to catch a glimpse of her, as I somehow proceeded to drag myself across to the other side of the road without using my left hand or my right leg. She was halfway up a heavily wooded hill where there were no buildings or trails. This was a section of the old psychiatric center where you'd rarely find hikers or joggers, even on a busy weekend.

It was completely out of place that anyone would be up there in those woods so early on a Monday morning. What was even more peculiar was the fact that the woman was impeccably dressed, wearing a beautiful white dress and fancy stiletto style high heels. The only thing that made any sense was perhaps she might have climbed up there to try to obtain cell phone signal so she could call for help. But where she came from remained a complete mystery. I didn't see any other car on the road, and it was very obvious that she could not have been a passenger in the truck.

In school they love to teach us about adrenalin and the superhuman effects it can have on our bodies during times like these. We've all heard the stories about panicking mothers lifting their automobiles clear off the ground to save their trapped children underneath. In my situation, the adrenalin allowed me to perform the unlikely, (and highly doubtful) feat of exiting the wreckage and traveling across the road. That feat was so unbelievable that I spent the better part of the next half hour trying to convince anyone who would listen that I was indeed the driver of the Jaguar.

It all started with the first police officer to arrive on the scene. Looking at the Jaguar and how crushed it appeared, compared to the more intact truck, he immediately concluded that I could only have been a passenger in the truck. When I insisted that I was the driver of the Jaguar, he concluded that I was merely in shock and talking gibberish.

Ironically, when the firemen and paramedics arrived, most of them turned their immediate attention toward rescuing the driver of the Jaguar!

The car was so mangled that it was impossible to tell that there was nobody inside. As a matter of fact, it was almost impossible to tell that it was once a Jaguar.

I tried my best to convince whoever would listen to me that they were wasting their time, because I was the lone occupant of the car. The fact that all four doors were jammed closed and all of the car's windows were still intact made the possibility of anyone escaping highly unlikely. Then I remembered the woman in the white dress and how she watched me escape from the car. I searched the accident scene for any sight of her, but she was nowhere to be found. I told one of the police officers how the woman who called 9-1-1 could confirm my story that I was the driver of the Jaguar. He gave me the strangest look as he informed me that there was no 9-1-1 call and how the news of the accident was reported by a school bus driver who called it in on his two-way radio. He made me start to doubt whether or not the image of that woman in the white dress was merely my mind playing tricks on me. I then had a very slight recollection of that shockwave causing havoc inside my skull right before I blacked out. It made me consider for the first time the possibility that I might have injured my head in the collision.

The fact that I have a very down-to-earth personality didn't support my claim either. Jaguars are symbols of wealth and prestige. Although I'm a workaholic who earns enough money to afford a Jaguar, (thanks to that great work ethic that was handed down to me), I don't come across with the snobby nose-in-the-air attitude that many people would expect a Jaguar owner to have. Jaguars are associated with what is commonly referred to as 'old money.' Out here on Long Island, (especially on the North Shore), we have our fair share of families with wealthy histories, but middle class or upper-middle class, at best would be used to describe our town in the pecking order of social classification. The bottom line is that there simply aren't many Jaguars on our streets.

The only thing that seemed more unlikely that a guy like me, who stood at five foot, eight inches, and weighed around two hundred pounds was able to escape that mangled pile of steel, (that was once a beautifully sleek Jaguar), is the thought that a guy like me could own a Jaguar in the first place. Anyone at the accident scene who entertained that notion immediately concluded that I was delusional.

So out came the 'Jaws of Life...'

I observed a set of paramedics working diligently to provide medical assistance to the still unconscious driver of the truck. Meanwhile, a group of firemen prepared to utilize the famous hydraulic tool known as the 'Jaws of Life' to pry open one of the Jaguar's doors.

The number of people on the scene was astonishing. What was previously a quiet deserted countryside road, was now overly crowded with rescue workers and countless observers, curious to see the fireman in action, as they attempted to retrieve the driver of the Jaguar from the wreckage.

As time passed, I started to notice that the rescuers paid less attention to me as I sat there on the side of the road with my injuries yet to be unattended to. And as even more time passed, so did my adrenalin rush. So much time had actually passed since anyone acknowledged my existence that I started to consider the possibility that maybe I died in that car wreck after all. We see this scenario played out in movies all the time, where a person dies in a car accident and then as a spirit observes his or her own accident scene.

Needless to say, there wasn't anyone on that road now more curious to see what the fireman would discover inside the Jaguar once the Jaws of Life granted them access, than me. It then all began to make perfect sense to me. The paramedics were swarming around the driver of the truck, yet despite my severe injuries, not one of them so much as took my pulse. There were countless policemen on the scene, yet not one of them asked me for my name or if there was someone in my family I would like them to contact. Then there was the cell phone lady from the hill. Surely she would have told someone how she saw me exit the vehicle. Yet once help began to arrive, she was nowhere to be found. The more that time passed the more I came to the logical conclusion-

I was dead.

When the Jaws of Life revealed what was left of the interior of the Jaguar, they surely were going to find my lifeless body. This was my new reality. This is what made the most sense. Just as I had calculated during that moment before impact, the collision was too great for any human to survive.

Blunt Force Trauma.

After extracting my body out of the car and on to a stretcher, it would be transported to a trauma center at a local hospital where an emergency room doctor would officially pronounce me dead. The next day an autopsy by the county medical examiner would reveal all of the internal damage caused by the freaking nasty shockwave. In addition to the ligament damage to my hand, foot and knee, they would soon discover severe injuries to many of my vital organs. But the real killer, the absolute cause of my death, will be determined by the autopsy to be damage to my brain stem from the shockwave.

I once read somewhere that brain injury is responsible for 50% of all deaths due to automobile accidents. The moment I felt that shockwave toss around the lobes of my brain I was   convinced that I would become part of that statistic. It would become official when the coroner writes the words "brain injury due to blunt force trauma – automobile accident" or something like that on my death certificate.

This was becoming my new reality, (as I sat there on the side of the road watching the expressions on each of the face of each fireman as they caught a glimpse of the contents of the Jaguar). I was certain that I had become a spectator to the scene of what was surely my own death. I watched their faces and waited for their reaction.

Waited for it…

And waited for it…

And then, all of a sudden, there it was. Their faces all told the same story. It was obvious when they looked into the cockpit of the car, that they did not like what they discovered. From their strange expressions, I could sense that they were clearly disappointed with themselves. I began to consider that my death was so horrific that the sight of it caused disbelief, even in the minds of rescue workers who see horrible deaths all of the time.

The vision froze their bodies. As a matter of fact, everyone at the accident scene appeared to freeze in time, as all eyes were glued toward the fireman staring into my car. It was if I was watching a movie and accidentally pressed the "pause" button. Everyone was silent and frozen for what felt like an eternity. All of our eyes continued to be glued upon the faces of those firemen. Almost simultaneously they raised their heads as I expected them to shake them in disappointment, but instead, one by one, they looked across the road directly at me sitting there crippled on the road. Right then I knew instantly what they saw inside the car…

It was empty, and they finally realized I had been telling the truth about who I was all along… the driver of the Jaguar.

Chapter 4

Childhood is supposed to be a time of innocence. When I was only eight years old, I was tormented in school with names like Pussy and Gaylord. Other choice labels were Putz, Geek, Homo, Freak, Moron, Dickhead, Queer, Weirdo and Dirtbag. As a result of this name-calling, I found there to be nothing innocent about my fellow third graders. Thanks to my Brooklyn origins, however, I had a pretty thick skin to help me tolerate the endless list of abusive names. The only one that really got under my skin was the name Faggot, (and Fag for short). It's a disgusting word that had no right being yelled across the schoolyard, scribbled across a desk, or whispered in the hallways.

I wasn't gay. I didn't look gay, nor did I act gay. I have always been a heterosexual who passionately worships and desires females. But none of that mattered, because my generation had a ridiculous obsession with homophobic profanities. Anyone who wasn't cool was at one time or another verbally attacked with horrific anti-gay slander, and the word faggot was the mother of them all. Just the sound of the word screams HATRED! That's why it became such a popular choice phrase. For the third-grade bullies, it had absolutely nothing at all to do with sexual orientation, but everything to do with how cruel the word sounded as it exited their lips.

Gay or not, being called a faggot by one of the popular kids, (with an audience listening), was one of the most degrading experiences a child in any era could endure.

I used to wish that I had been born just three or four years sooner, because the generation before mine was so much nicer than mine. If this makes any sense, they were a generation, who knew a generation, who were the last of the hippie generation. Enough of the 'Make Peace/Not War' mentality had been passed on to them to make them regard bullying as a complete waste of energy.

Typically speaking, it is usually the upperclassmen that are the culprits responsible for dishing out the grief to the younger students. That wasn't the case at all when I went to school. Even when we grew older, the generation before mine was only concerned with drinking beer, smoking pot and having sex while listening to great music. There was no time left in that agenda for harassing the weaker kids in the neighborhood.

On the other hand, harassment was one of the most popular pastimes of my generation.

The thugs I had to call classmates were the complete polar opposites of hippies, and the humiliation they dished out wasn't just limited to verbal abuse either. The physical punishment was brutal. I've taken my fair share of punches as well. In the beginning I tried with all my might to fight back, only to learn that it makes the situation worse for someone who is out-sized and out-numbered, (especially when the other party has home field advantage). Over time

I learned that the best course of action was to escape and run away as quickly as possible.

Speaking of home field advantage, even the school personnel were severely biased toward their own. I remember how furious my parents were when I was suspended from school once for allegedly biting another child. The school officials mysteriously overlooked the fact that the injury took place as the other kid was charging at me like a bull in an all-out sprint, while I was looking the other way. The accident report seemed to have left out the part that the bite mark was on top of the other child's scalp and that he stood at least eighteen inches taller than me. My parents were never given an explanation as to why twelve eyewitnesses were never permitted to state how they saw the bully cut his scalp on my front teeth, while I was standing there minding my own business. We later learned that the school principal was the bully's uncle! Even if the entire incident was caught on film, I still would have been held responsible while the other kid got to walk away without even a warning. That was my first lesson in how easy favoritism can out-trump justice.

Despite what many people believe, a child doesn't become numb or immune to repeated bouts of abuse. Getting abused in succession is like getting stabbed in an open wound over and over again. When I was a child, society failed to recognize bullying as a form of child abuse. Not sure why that was so. Pain is pain, whether it's dished out by an adult, or by another child. That was the reality for those of us who were victims. It's probably also the reason why most of today's school administrations take a well-needed hard stance against bullying.

There were often times when I felt as if my enemies were taking battlefield tactics right from the pages of Sun Tzu's *The Art of War*. For instance, I had to deal with the element of not knowing where or how their next attack would be coming. Sometimes they would jump me from behind as I was exiting the school. Other times I would be ambushed in the boy's room, or on the way home from school. The element of surprise was one of the many dilemmas I faced on a daily basis.

Between the physical and emotional abuse I thought the torture was the worse that it could get, but that was until I was given a taste of how nasty psychological abuse can be. When people think of the bullying that can take place in the third grade, they usually think of the classic schoolyard pranks like Wedgies, Noogies, "Kick-Me" signs and Wet Willies. When they think of the worst pranks they usually think of something like the Atomic Wedgie, (a wedgie where the elastic band of the victim's underwear is pulled so hard up their back, that it's stretched over the top of their head while they are still wearing the underwear). As painful and humiliating such experiences might be, it's not half as bad as the suffering that results from psychological abuse.

For instance, one semester I had to purposely lose ten points on every quiz I took, because I completed them using ink instead of pencil. I was well aware that the teacher would impose a ten-point penalty for not using a pencil, but I had no other choice but to write my answers in ink, because otherwise one of my devious classmates would sneak into the classroom during lunchtime to erase and change all of my answers! I had to settle for grades in the 70s and 80s to avoid failing the class. That's just one example of some of the sick mind games the bullies would play on me.

Another classic head trip was the time someone framed me for stealing stuff like Barbie Dolls and lip gloss from the girls in the school. The secret culprit would hide stolen items in my desk and backpack so I would get the blame. After this went on for several weeks, some irate parents went ballistic, thinking I was some sort of kleptomaniac, with a sick fetish for girl's possessions. I was certain that I was going to be expelled from school, because it was impossible to prove that I was being framed. Lucky for me, the idiot who was doing the framing was caught in the act of placing more stolen items in my desk. The sick thing was, they found a pair of girl's panties in his gym locker, along with the remainder of the missing items. Yet somehow, I was still the one who everyone remembered as being the sicko.

I learned very quickly that we live in a world where perception becomes reality. That's part of what makes psychological abuse so effective. The bullies were obviously well aware of the fact that the world is often too lazy to pursue the real truth, so they often grasp on to and believe the first explanation that makes any sort of sense. For me, that meant becoming the object of irrational blame and hostility, (aka the scapegoat).

Those were some very confusing times for me. I often cried myself to sleep, because I did not understand what I had done to deserve the unbearable emotional and physical pain. I was raised to believe that we should always treat each other with respect. Just like my old neighborhood, the majority of the families in my new neighborhood were church-going people.

Everyone was familiar with how clearly the Bible teaches concepts, such as 'Do unto others as you would have others do unto you, as well as Love thy neighbor as thyself.' Yet each day I was being tortured by classmates who clearly showed absolutely no regard for what they should have learned from their religion. Naturally, not a single adult in their lives suspected them of being anything other than perfect model citizens.

I guess all of us could have been accused of living double lives, if you took a look at how we acted around our families. At home, kids like me would act all happy, like our lives were perfect. And at their homes, the kids who were kicking our asses on a daily basis were acting like perfect little angels. As much as I needed help, I found it utterly embarrassing to admit to anyone that I was being bullied.

I'm not sure why, but on some strange level abuse victims seem to blame ourselves for the pain that is inflicted upon us. It's clear to me now that none of it was my fault, (especially since I made every attempt possible to try to fit in and keep a low profile). But things were not so clear when I was in the middle of all of that turmoil.

I may have been able to do a decent job of concealing my sorrow from most of the adult world, but not all of the adults in my life were fooled. I recall one Sunday afternoon, one of my great-uncles was able to detect that I had been spending a good amount of time rubbing tears out of my eyes. When I realized my cover was up, I expected the old-timer to offer up some sort of words of wisdom or comfort, but instead he gave me this most bizarre lecture on how I needed to stop rubbing my eyes, because if I didn't stop rubbing them, I would go blind! It sounded to me like an old wives' tale that was created to stop young children from rubbing their eyes, by scaring the shit out of them. I was usually interested in hearing the old-timers share their folklore, but there was something about that particular lecture that just struck a nerve with me.

The only other time I can remember when an adult in my life was made aware of my troubles, was when the abuse had escaladed so out of control that I had no choice left but to ask my mom for help. I gave her the exact time and location of my next scheduled ass kicking, so she could intervene. Naturally, she was really good at intimidating the bullies, along with the adults who enabled them. The problem for me was that she was too good. Her involvement added the term Momma's Boy to my ever-growing list of titles. If you stop and think about it, you realize what a screwed-up world we live in. My peers found nothing wrong with eight kids, (twice the size of me), pouncing on my body on a daily basis, but the moment I asked my mom for the help, (that the adults in the school refused to provide), I was the one who they considered to be an unfair fighter. I became known as the kid who had his mother fight his battles for him. And that added, yet another reason why that target on my back was never going to disappear.

It seems like a miracle that all of that stress didn't make me physically ill. It was actually rare for me to get sick as a child, but when I did I often had a very high fever. I always knew when I had a fever, because I would lie in bed feeling this odd sensation like my body was swelling like a balloon. I could not fall asleep with a fever, no matter how exhausted or weak I was. The best I could do was fade into this zombie-like state, where I was barely aware of my consciousness. I would then have the same reoccurring daydream of balloon-like shapes inflating. It's extremely difficult to explain. All I know is that this only occurred when I had a high fever.

The remedy back then for reducing a high fever was a rubbing alcohol sponge bath.

When the alcohol evaporated from the skin, it gave a cooling sensation. Back then there wasn't much concern for alcohol poisoning from the fumes, or from rapid absorption through the skin. At that point nobody even realized that the rubbing alcohol could have caused some serious neurological or cardiac problems. The only thing I found refreshing about having a fever, was that it made it very obvious that something was wrong. There was no question that you were sick, and it was easy to measure when you were better. No mystery involved at all. I wish I could say the same about going blind the way that I did.

The early stage of my vision loss was typical of any child who learned of the need to wear glasses. Like many children, it was a teacher who was the first person to suspect that there was something wrong with my eyesight. She sent me down to the school's nurse, because she didn't like the way I was having difficulty reading the blackboard. The nurse administered one of those simple eyesight exams, that all of us in the modern world are familiar with. It's the same old routine where they make us cover one eye and read the eye chart with the other eye starting with that giant 'E.' Then we have to work our way down the chart until we reach that 20/20 finish line. In my case, I never made it that far. I reached a point where I was unable to distinguish the G's from the O's, or the H's from the A's. My heart raced as I considered the possibility that there was some validity behind my uncle's earlier warning about eye rubbing.

The nurse scribbled a short message on a note and instructed me to have my parents bring that note to my eye doctor. It was very difficult for anyone without a medical degree to read her handwriting, (never mind decipher her message to the doctor). The only line that was legible was one that said "OD 20/40." The problem was that I didn't have an eye doctor. To make matters worse, it was the middle of December. So between locating a reputable doctor in the area and booking an appointment for me as a new patient, we waited about four weeks before that nurse's note could be properly addressed. In the meantime, my teacher moved me to a desk toward the front of the classroom. Naturally this gave my classmates yet another excuse to pick on me, because anyone who sat in the front of the class was labeled a 'teacher's pet.'

In regards to the content of that note, I still remember a great debate that broke out during the holidays over the meaning of that code, OD 20/40. It was assumed that the code meant that the nurse thought that I had 20/40 vision. But still to this day, there seems to be a great amount of confusion in our society about what it means to have 20/20 vision, versus other measurements, such as 20/40 vision, and so on. The most popular misconception seems to be a belief that the first number is the measurement of the vision in the left eye, and the second measurement is the vision in the right eye. The fact that I told everyone that I only had trouble reading the eye chart with my right eye, may have helped support that misconception too.

It was entertaining, however, observing grownups arguing like children over this. The authoritative figures in our lives preach to us how we should not behave. Then, a silly debate like this comes along, and one-by-one, each of them displays the exact behavior that they warned us about. In this situation the arguments got so deep, that my eye doctor's appointment became more about what the heck OD 20/40 meant, than why I had it in the first place.

The only thing that everyone was able to agree upon during that debate, was that our schooling and the medical field did a really lousy job of teaching us how to decipher the whole 20/20 vision scale. The only person, who was even remotely close to figuring it out, was one of my grandmothers who worked at the Veterans Administration hospital during one of the wars. She insisted that the number 20 in the formula stood for twenty feet, because when she was asked to set up a room to administer eye examinations to the vets, she remembered that she had to measure off twenty feet with a tape measure.

My grandmother was in fact, right on target. The eye doctor later taught us how the entire system of measuring eyesight revolves around what people can normally see from twenty feet away. That is the standard upon which all vision is measured against. That is why the first number, when recording a patient's vision is always the number 20. The second number is actually the number that represents a patient's vision. 20/20 vision means that at twenty feet away a patient can read what a patient with normal eyesight is expected to read at twenty feet.

This measurement is taken for each eye independently and then written out as either Oculus (eye) Dexter (right), or OD for the right eye, and Oculus (eye) Sinister (left), or OS for the left eye. So what my school nurse was indicating with her code OD 20/40, was that the best line that I could read on the chart with my right eye at twenty feet away, was equal to the line that a person with normal vision could read at FORTY feet away! So someone with 20/40 vision has TWICE as poor vision as someone with 20/20.

After the examination the eye doctor went on to explain to us that his findings agreed with the nurse's. He didn't volunteer any medical explanation for the cause of my vision loss and I was too frightened, (and embarrassed), to ask if rubbing my eyes too much could have been the reason. So, I never found out that day whether or not it was true that eye rubbing can cause vision loss. All I remember was within a few days his office crafted a pair of glasses for me with corrective lens for my right eye, and a clear dummy lens for my left eye. The glasses allowed me to once again read that 20/20 line on the eye chart from twenty feet away out of both eyes.

That examination gave no reason to suspect that there was anything unusual about my vision loss. Becoming one of the millions of children who wear eyeglasses was not exactly cause for alarm either, but on some strange level I sensed that something just wasn't quite right.

The funny thing about vision loss is that you really don't take much notice when you lose it gradually over time. That's mainly because you aren't aware of what you can't see, (or what you're missing). I learned this the first time I walked to school wearing those new eyeglasses. I became fascinated with viewing all of the tiny nooks and crannies in the sidewalk. It's amazing how incredible the world looks through a new pair of glasses. It's the tiny little details that I was missing by having 20/40 vision in one eye. Even though my other eye could still see 20/20, the images being projected to my brain simply were not the same without the stereovision that only good vision through two eyes could provide.

I was pretty excited about wearing those new glasses too. But that excitement ended before I even reached the school that morning. I thought I had it as tough as it could get, being forever labeled the nerdy new kid and all, but I soon found out that the only thing worse than being a nerdy new kid, was being a nerdy new kid with glasses. The name-calling and physical punishment from my peers started a block away from the school. The closer I walked toward the school, the more it intensified.

I thought there was no name crueler than faggot. That was until I felt what it was like to be called a 'Four-Eyed Faggot.' For a moment there I thought something was going wrong with the new glasses, because that crisp incredible vision was starting to become blurry. Then I realized my eyes were becoming watery, because I could no longer hold back the tears. I don't know why the cool kids were so obsessed with bashing anyone who wore glasses. It's tough enough to deal with the nuisance of wearing them and all of the discomfort and hardship that goes along with it, without being made fun of for wearing them.

Talk about mixed emotions. Part of me was ecstatic over how well the glasses were able to correct my vision, while another part of me despised them for all of the added stress and constant heckling I received from wearing them. I somehow managed to put up with it for two solid weeks. Then, like a miracle, it all ended on the night of February 24th, 1976. You see, that's the night that Fonzie learned that he needed to wear glasses too!

Fonzie, (or The Fonz), is the nickname for Arthur Fonzarelli, a fictional character that was played by the actor Henry Winkler in the sitcom *Happy Days* (arguably the most popular primetime sitcom of all time). The show was so influential, that in many ways it helped define my generation. Both on the show and in real life, nobody wanted to be a nerd. Fonzie got all of the chicks. Fonzie had all of the friends. So naturally, everyone wanted to be cool like The Fonz.

Little did anyone, (including the show's writers) know how that episode was going to instantly transform wearing glasses into something that is now cool. It all started when Fonzie became uncharacteristically clumsy. He was obviously not his perfect cool self. He developed severe headaches too. Eventually it was suggested that he might need glasses. After a visit with the character Ralph Malph's father, (who was an eye doctor), Fonzie was able to read the eye chart perfectly with his left eye, but his right eye had poor vision. Sound familiar? His clumsiness and headaches were attributed to the imbalance in his vision.

Up until that moment only geeks and nerds wore eye glasses. Then Fonzie sent a message to the world that cool people can wear glasses too. And just like that, in one episode, a fictional character on primetime TV was able to accomplish what preachers, schools and parents had been trying to accomplish for decades. Eyeglasses were now in.

Sales of new eyeglasses soared around my neighborhood. Even people with perfect vision started wearing eyeglasses as a fashion accessory.

I am forever grateful for the timing of that episode, because the preceding two weeks were simply hell. I remember watching *Happy Days* every Tuesday night with my family, and often suspecting that we would somehow benefit from the way the world idolized The Fonz. I just never would have guessed that it would have been in that manner. I was hopeful that my peers would have caught on to the way Henry Winkler's character held such high moral standards. I was wishful that more people in the world would stick up for those in need and treat others with respect as well as Fonzie did. Even though those wishes never came true, it is still pretty amazing how thanks to The Fonz, starting on February 24th, 1976, I never received an ounce of grief about wearing glasses ever again. It didn't solve my bullying problem, but it was surely a welcomed step in the right direction.

I made other progress that same year when I managed to find two organizations where I could make new friends and be treated with dignity and respect; the school band and *The Boy Scouts of America*. Even though I knew that my new enrollment in each of these groups would elevate my name even higher on the bullies' hit lists, it was a risk I was more than happy to take. You see, I knew that I would find sanctuary within the confines of both of the groups. The old notion, 'there is safety in numbers' held true, even for those regarded as band geeks and scout freaks. So, for the very first time since moving to Long Island, (within the ranks of fellow musicians and outdoor enthusiasts), I could be myself without being on the defensive and in constant fear.

Being an avid music lover, it was inevitable that I would pursue an interest in learning to read sheet music and play an instrument. The alto saxophone was my choice. The instrument's 23 keys, fancy brass curves and wooden reed intrigued me. It looked extremely complicated to play. I found the idea of being able to master an instrument that others feared, to be most appealing. It was a challenge that I needed to pursue.

They say that learning to play music can enhance a person's math skills. I think they make this claim, because reading and playing music is mostly one giant math problem. Math has always been my best subject, so I was pleasantly surprised to discover how learning to play music came naturally to me. I also loved how friendly my fellow musicians were toward me. Being a band member provides some great lessons in teamwork, accountability and discipline, but it was still fun and rewarding, (even when we had to endure long strenuous practice sessions, or when we had to perform the most challenging musical scores). I particularly loved the on-stage performances. The limelight, along with the roar of the crowd, was the perfect remedy to help heal my beaten and battered ego.

I found my other salvation in scouting. It was a place where I could learn an abundance of useful skills, while at the same time, form solid friendships. Actually, many of my fellow scouts would become my best childhood friends. And just like the complexity of the saxophone, I found the long list of requirements for advancement through the ranks incredibly appealing. I was fascinated by the fact that less than two percent of the millions of scouts ever make it all the way to the top rank of *Eagle Scout.*

They say 'Once an Eagle, Always an Eagle,' because the title stays with the person for life. Neil Armstrong, Steven Spielberg and a handful of Nobel Prize winners, top the list of the most notable Eagle Scouts. Setting out to accomplish something so tough that ninety-eight percent of those who try fail, was a journey I decided I needed to go on, (no matter how impossible it seemed). I wanted, (and needed), to prove to myself that I could be among the elite. Looking through the scout handbook it became apparent that mastering the required skills meant becoming efficient in a large spectrum of topics. Of course there was the core stuff that we all think of like camping, first aid and citizenship, but there was also a long list of badges in all sorts of other subject areas.

Earning the prestigious rank of Eagle Scout, means earning the right to be regarded as a person who has broad intellectual interests, and who is admired for being accomplished in multiple areas of expertise. Just the idea that I could be regarded as a person, (instead of a pile of shit, lying in the schoolyard dirt that kids took turns spitting on), was appealing enough to me.

The idea that I could become someone who would be admired for being accomplished was a simply amazing fantasy, no matter how far-fetched it seemed.

The moment I realized that this was who I wanted to become was the moment I started taking back control of my life.

Chapter 5

When I was in the back of that ambulance after the car accident, I had the most random thought flash through my mind. I recalled how shortly after I started getting my childhood in order, I started to view the world as a philosopher would. I spent most of that journey to the hospital recalling how I first learned to look for the deeper meanings that lie buried behind seemingly ordinary events. My memory was a bit fuzzy, but I did recall how even though adolescence was an extremely challenging time for all of us, I had a knack for using highly rational thoughts to get both my friends and myself through whatever chaos came our way.

In many ways you cannot deny the irony. For someone who went through a hell of a time during childhood, it seems most unlikely that I would have had it easiest during adolescence. Go figure! All I know is that I quickly started to discover the many benefits that can arise from deep thoughts and the development of complex theories.

I enjoyed being a student of life with an open mind. I don't know why I started to look at the world differently, or how I even knew how to look at it through philosophical eyes. All I do remember is that I loved it. From what I was

77

told, I was good at it too. I also found that although I was not alone in my desire to analyze the world, I was unique in the way I could still share my theories with my peers and my elders in ways that they all could easily relate.

You see, most teenagers, (and adults), who set out on the journey to discover the meaning of life, (and to unlock all of its secrets), usually find themselves so deeply entangled in their own thoughts, that they lose their ability to fit in within society. Outcasts and weirdoes are the common labels for most teenage philosophers. This goes way beyond the traditional schoolyard socio-classifications of cool vs. nerd.

I once had a friend who was so obsessed with analyzing life, that he literally lost his mind doing it. That might be the extreme, but every generation does have its share of strange loners, who might be highly knowledgeable about the ways of the world, but nobody will ever have the opportunity to know it.

I guess in my case, (after years of being on the receiving end of humiliation for being perceived as being different), I developed a talent for knowing how to blend in. As a result, I learned how to be a modern-day philosopher without alienating myself from the rest of the civilized world. This allowed me to practice my desire for higher thinking, while at the same time maintain the ability to share my theories in simple laymen's terminology that almost anyone could grasp and understand. So, in a very short period of time, (and at a relatively young age, I might add), I became known as being a person to turn to for reliable advice, on everything from relationships to finances.

Now that I think about it, looking back on being in the ambulance that day, in all that pain, (yet thinking about something from my childhood as abstract as this), was a pretty peculiar thing to be doing. What made it stranger was how I continued to recollect my adolescent self, (as if I was thinking of myself as a person in the past tense), as if my life had terminated that day on that road that winding abandoned psychiatric hospital road. However, the physical agony I felt every time the ambulance hit another pothole was a renewed confirmation that I was still very much alive. Yet as the minutes ticked away, (and the more time progressed), the more it become increasingly obvious to me that something was actually much more terribly wrong with my mind, than with all of my bones, ligaments, skin and muscle combined.

For instance, about halfway through the journey to the hospital, I swear that I heard my wife in the ambulance with us. I know for a fact that I was alone that morning, yet I could clearly hear her jokingly ask the ambulance driver if she could press the magical button that he utilized to automatically switch all of the upcoming traffic lights from red to green. The more I listened, however, the more I started to think about how I was probably completely out of my mind.

Worse yet, what if something was actually wrong with my mind? The possibility that I sustained some sort of brain damage was a thought that was too intense to deal with, after all that I had already been through that morning. So to shield myself, (I utilized an old defensive tactic that I perfected back in the days when the schoolyard bullies took turns beating the crap out of me), I buried myself deep enough in my thoughts to make me numb to the real world around me.

So instead of struggling with the dilemma that my wife's presence in the ambulance was a hallucination, (or that she was really there and I had simply lost all memory of how she came to be by my side), I turned my attention back toward my adolescence and how much I enjoyed sharing my passion for philosophical thinking with others. I thought about how the more frequent people turned to me for answers to their complex questions, the more I started to realize that I possessed an incredible knack for feeling in my heart what was right or wrong.

I also discovered that I had this remarkable ability for sensing when something good or bad was about to happen. You can call it intuition, or you can call it a coincidence. In some cultures they might even have called it some sort of sorcery. But everyone knew that whatever you wanted to call it, there was no denying that my words of wisdom as a child were remarkably accurate.

And, as I grew into adulthood, I carried the same philosophical interest right there with me. Through the years I may have gotten caught up in the demands of raising a family and excelling at my career, however, I still manage to find time for analyzing the world around us, and lending others some very solid advice. My quest for the meaning of life may not be as intense as it was when I was a teenager, but I never lost my desire, (or ability), to unlock those magical secret lessons out there waiting for us to discover, during the course of our everyday lives.

For instance, just the other day I was listening to my youngest daughter's riding instructor, and I found an incredible hidden meeting in her lesson about controlling a horse through an equitation course.

She was explaining how riders often worry too much about the jumps in the course. They become so obsessed with clearing the hurdles that their ride ends up looking awkward and their timing gets thrown way off as a result. She went on to explain how focusing on the riding that takes place between the jumps, (instead of putting so much emphasis upon the jumps themselves), will make the trip through the course look much more fluid. By concentrating on the flatwork, (the skills required to ride the horse properly on the flat parts of the course), and getting it down like clockwork, the jumps will not be an issue, because they will become almost automatic. When the ride in between the jumps is as good as clockwork, the jumps will fit right in.

I enjoyed hearing the pro's advice in the riding ring. She got me thinking about how living life is much like riding through one of those courses. Just like on the course, life is full of a bunch of hurdles. Sometimes the obstacles are small, unexpected dilemmas. More often than not, however, they are full-blown catastrophes. The periods of time in our lives in between the obstacles are equivalent to the flats on the jumping course. With that in mind, the philosopher in me loves the idea of taking that valuable lesson from the riding ring and applying it to the way we handle the obstacles in life. I realized that just like on the jump course, the more we concentrate upon making sure that our lives run like clockwork in the flats, the better prepared we will be to make it over life's obstacles.

It made me think of all of the people out there who become so paranoid and obsessed with worrying about all of the bad things that could possibly happen in the future, that the anxiety that their obsessing creates, actually stops them from living and enjoying their lives in the present. It also made me think of how much a wooden jump actually resembles a roadblock, or a barricade. As a matter of fact, a hurdle is sometimes only a hurdle through the eyes of a jumper. To everyone else it symbolizes an unsurpassable barrier.

Getting back to the catastrophes in life, nobody knows better than a runt of the litter how much they are guaranteed to happen. Anyone who has ever been bullied repeatedly will tell you that what matters most is how a person picks themselves up and carries on after life gives them a good beating. This goes back to the concept of never letting anyone, or anything get the best of you. It also includes another valuable lesson taken from horsemanship:

If you fall off a horse you must get back on right away.

When the schoolyard bullies were beating the hell out of me, the only thing that was important to me was how soon I could get back on my feet and pretend that the beating never happened in the first place. That is all that was on my mind. I felt that same way as I was lying on the stretcher in the ambulance. As horrendous as the accident was, the thing that was really on my mind was how quickly the doctors might be able to mend my broken body, and in turn how fast my insurance company could act to replace my wife's destroyed Jaguar.

I knew deep down inside that those were the thoughts I needed to grasp onto in order to remain strong. Just like in the schoolyard, any admission of vulnerability would have been the equivalent of waiving a white flag. Still, my body ached so badly from my injuries. I also became increasingly aware of a brace that the paramedics must have strapped around my neck. I must have been wearing it the entire time. It puzzled me how it took so long for me to realize how insanely tight the brace was clamped in place to completely immobilize my upper spine. I also still had that nagging feeling that something was also terribly wrong with my mind.

Inside my head there was this uncomfortable silence during moments when I expected there to be thoughts. It's not that I couldn't think, it was more like I felt like something was missing or off. Next time you are in an automobile, tune the radio to your favorite music station. Then play around with the adjustments on the system by turning the Fade all the way to Rear and the Balance control all the way to Left. Then change the Treble and Base levels as low as they will go. If you listen to a few of your favorite songs with the stereo set this way, you can start to gain an understanding of how my mind was functioning after the collision with the truck. You can still recognize the songs, but your senses suggest to you that something is off.

Traumatic brain injury can affect a victim in thousands of different ways, and in unlimited combinations. It usually breaks our hearts when we see people who suffer paralysis on the right sides of their bodies, and who at the same time exhibit a diminished ability to communicate. This is usually how we picture someone who has brain damage. Most of the time those symptoms are caused by widespread damage to the left hemisphere of the brain. But what if a victim's injuries are confined to smaller, more precise areas of the brain that control less obvious functions? For instance, do you think anyone other than the victim would even notice if damage was sustained to small parts of the frontal lobe located in the Neocortex that control, (among other things), problem solving, reasoning, judgment and memory?

I can tell you from my firsthand experience that the answer is undoubtedly 'No.' Perhaps someone might notice if a victim's motor skills are deficient, but will the world even care if a victim loses his ability to feel altruism, guilt, embarrassment, or any of the other higher emotions like empathy, sympathy or shame? As a matter of fact, unless a patient demonstrates clear signs of head injury, (like a bump or cut on their head), or complains of symptoms that are commonly associated with head injuries, it's unlikely that the attending physician will even conduct a neurological examination on the patient. Before I even arrived at the hospital, I was already aware how I was going to have a really tough time convincing anyone that there was anything wrong with my mind, seeing as how I didn't have any bumps or bruises on my actual head.

Brain scans are costly procedures. Thanks to the limitations of our healthcare system, even severe trauma patients are not given MRI's or Cat Scans of the head, without valid suspicion of possible brain injury. However, I was well aware of the awkward silence in my head that somehow must have been a result of the accident, but didn't know how to explain or to prove it. I must have complained fifteen times to the paramedics that something was wrong with my mind. But since I was able to recite my name, count backward from ten and wiggle my toes, the only comment written in my chart to relay to the hospital staff about my mental state was how I was most likely in shock.

Not being able to convince a healthcare provider that something is wrong, (when you know that something obviously is), can be incredibly frustrating at first, and then downright depressing afterward. In my case, it was immediately obvious to me that I was missing my ability to sustain higher thinking. For instance, as I accepted the notion that I could not allow the collision to cause any major interruptions in my life, I had no problem remembering and understanding the 'get right back on the horse concept.' I also had no problem recalling how in the past I would never allow any setbacks to interfere with my desire to succeed. And although at that point in time, I had not yet had the pleasure of overhearing the riding instructor's advice on how to conquer the jumps in a course like they weren't even there, I did recall that I had been following a similar theory that had to do with the importance of building up, (and sustaining), momentum in life.

I knew that it was extremely inspirational advice that in the past had helped many of us overcome our own personal hurdles in life and threatened to disrupt our plans. The only problem was, I could not remember the exact concept, where it came from, or any of the details on how exactly it had helped any of us in the past. The more I attempted to recall those thoughts, the more I started to get dizzy during that ambulance ride. I knew the wise saying, (that I had difficulty remembering), had something to do with goal setting. I was also able to recall how awesome the concept made me feel whenever I read it. I just lost the ability to recall those words of wisdom to the front of my mind. The more I tried to retrieve it from memory, the more frustrated I felt. I could remember reading it. I was even thinking how it had something to do with mountains, or shooting stars, or something, but I wasn't exactly sure.

I gave it one last shot before I developed what felt like a horrible migraine, and the only other thing I could recall was that it included a phrase about snake pits and outer space. Then, in an instant, my mind went to a very dark place full of confusion and frustration. For the first time in my life, I truly understood the meaning of the adjectives dumbfounded, stupefied, and all of their synonyms. I also, for the first time (in a very long time), found myself feeling absolutely zero motivation.

Soon my attention turned toward the beeping sound of the ambulance backing up and the cold swoosh of outside air that entered the cab of the vehicle as the rear doors were opened. At that point, the only thing I could think about was the ordeal of having to provide my prior medical history. When a person like me, with a long complicated medical history, it can be extremely frustrating having to constantly recite the details when we meet new medical providers. There was never a time when I felt that frustration more than when that ambulance brought me to the trauma unit at the university medical center. When you arrive at a hospital emergency room you are usually first greeted by a triage nurse. It's her responsibility to do an early assessment of your injuries, health history and determine the level of urgency your visit requires (compared to the other patients who are also waiting for medical assistance). When the triage nurse asked me if I ever had any surgeries, her question overwhelmed me. I felt this way partly because I was almost too exhausted to speak, but mostly because I found myself having difficulty remembering how to answer the question.

I was aware that I had undergone over a dozen surgeries since I was a teenager. But other than my eye surgeries, I couldn't remember the reason for any of the others. My heart started to race and I became nervous and uneasy. Now I really feared the possibility that there might be something seriously wrong with my mind. I initially thought that my ego was going to struggle with the embarrassment of looking like an idiot who couldn't even remember my own medical history. The odd thing was I had no feeling about it. That worried me even more, because a better part of my consciousness knew that I was supposed to feel embarrassment or shame.

Instead, I just lied there asking myself "what the hell was wrong with me?"

I could clearly remember how I often had to spend as much as thirty minutes explaining my medical history in detail during my past hospital visits. I also remember repeating and answering the same questions again for everyone who approached my hospital bed with my chart in their hands and a stethoscope around their neck. Reciting my medical history had always been second nature to me. In some sick demented way I was proud of my surgeries in much the same way that a decorated soldier is proud of his battle wounds. I even recalled how I had a system to help me remember all of my surgeries by starting with the scars on my feet, and then moving up to my legs, until I worked my way up through the rest of my body, and to the top of my head. I remembered the routine, yet I could not remember any of the specific surgeries.

The curiosity was killing me. My right leg was immobilized due to the new injuries that I sustained in the accident, but I was free to move my left leg. The only problem was that I was far too weak to lift it high enough for me to inspect it for any old scars that could give me the slightest clue of the memories I somehow could not retrieve. Without asking the reason why, the very nice triage nurse was kind enough to lift my left foot so that I could get a good look. Clear as day I saw a surgical scar on the left side of the ankle and what appeared to be a much older one across the front of my shin. Yet viewing those scars had no effect on my memory loss, I still had no clue when, where, or why I had to have those surgeries performed.

I didn't think that the horrible morning could have gotten any worse, (but I thought wrong). I remembered so well how those blank medical history forms usually had very limited space provided to list prior surgeries. I knew how frustrating it could be if the person writing the information had large penmanship, because it was not uncommon to see them run out of room before they even finished documenting the surgeries I had performed below the knees. I remembered quite well, how it often took additional pieces of paper by the time we reached my eye surgeries. Yet it made my head pound whenever I tried to recall the details about any of the procedures.

My memory loss startled me. I tried to explain it to my caretakers, but I had neither the energy nor the stamina to mumble more than a few words at a time without losing my breath. When I was finally able to exert myself enough to string together more than one sentence, it was so exhausting that I actually lost consciousness. Eventually I woke up to the sound of my wife's comforting voice speaking to someone about my eyes, but I was too weak to open my eyes to see whom she was speaking to. I could hear her explaining how I had three cornea transplants. This reminded me how I could usually anticipate a pause in the conversation whenever a doctor learned this about me for the first time.

Those conversations always went the same way. First I mention that I lost my vision due to a disease called Keratoconus. Then the doctor pretends to know what the disease is. I always find it entertaining how often so many physicians, (sometimes very prestigious ones too), are so egotistical, that they can't admit that they don't have a clue what the heck Keratoconus is. Usually the first giveaway is seeing them attempt to spell the name of the disease with the letter C, instead of the letter K. Watching them flip through the pages of their pocket medical dictionaries was another telltale sign.

I guess it must be some sort of medical doctor pride thing that prevents them from being able to admit that their years of practice and schooling failed to provide them with adequate education on this particular disease. But, unless a doctor is an eye specialist, or worked some shifts in a hospital's ophthalmology department when they were completing their residency, they shouldn't feel inadequate for not knowing about Keratoconus. The disease only affects around one in every 2000 people. That's less than $1/10^{th}$ of the population, so they shouldn't fault themselves for not knowing about a disease that does not affect 99.9% of their patients. At some point in time, someone influential in the medical field must have grown tired of saying the name Keratoconus, so he gave the disorder the nickname KC. That's fine with me, because even after all of these years, I still sometimes mistakenly misspell it. But, as I continued to listen to my wife describe my surgeries, I was even having difficulty remembering the simple initials, KC.

Not good. Those two words became the undertone for not only the way I felt physically, but also for the way I felt about the notion that I might have something seriously wrong with my mind. Just as I had anticipated, I failed to convince any of the doctors in the hospital that I sustained any sort of injury to my head. The only satisfaction I received, was finally learning what that burnt powder taste was that had been annoying the hell out of me ever since the collision. One nice physician's assistant at the hospital explained to me that it was either cornstarch, or talcum powder that was used by the manufacturer of the airbag to keep the airbag lubricated and pliable. Apparently all airbags release this powder when they are deployed. I found this news to be both comforting and disturbing. It was nice to finally know the source of that burnt powder, yet it annoyed me that I had no recollection of the airbag exploding in my face whatsoever. It made me curious as to what else I might not have been remembering.

The world surely works in mysterious ways. It never ceases to amaze me how time after time I am constantly being reminded how everything happens for a reason. Sometimes the lessons to be learned are quite obvious. Other times they don't reveal their true meaning until years, (or even decades), later. For instance, most people, when faced with the possibility that they might have sustained a head injury, have very little past experiences to help them form rational thoughts about the situation. I, on the other hand, had just spent the better part of the ten years prior to that moment caring for my wife and coordinating her medical care, after she miraculously survived two incredibly risky brain surgeries to clip a cerebral aneurysm that was located in the worst possible location on her carotid artery.

Needless to say, I was all too familiar with the symptoms and complications associated with head injury and trauma to the brain. And, not only was I aware of it, but I had actually lived it. That is how I knew something was seriously wrong. It's also why I knew that no doctor was going to take me seriously, no matter how hard I tried. In their eyes, I was just another paranoid lunatic patient. My vital signs were stable. My face and head looked remarkably in good shape in comparison to the rest of my body, (which was pretty banged up). Had I not complained about memory loss and the funny feeling in my head, chances are I probably would not have even been given the standard neurological examination.

The test is not too complicated to administer, but it does require a great deal of intelligence, patience and razor-sharp observational skills on the part of the physician. I've watched as it was administered to my wife dozens of times. It consists of a series of straightforward questions and simple tests that provide some very crucial information about the functioning of the brain, as well as the entire nervous system. The standard neurological examination is usually administered whenever there is even the slightest suspicion of injury to the brain, or any of the intricate components of the nervous system. It's an extremely inexpensive method to assess what might be wrong.

The test's major shortcoming, (from what I've witnessed firsthand), is that the result it produces are often only as good as the person administering the examination. More often than not, in a hospital setting, (especially in an emergency room), the neurological examination is administered by an intern or resident, instead of an experienced neurologist. Many people do not realize that an intern is someone in their first year after graduating medical school, and a resident is usually someone in their second, third- or fourth-year post graduation.

I totally understand how the success of the world's healthcare system depends upon providing newly licensed doctors opportunities to practice their skills, so they can make mistakes and learn from them. I just don't understand why the system allows them to practice without supervision. With all of the money Americans contribute toward the cost of healthcare, the least we should expect in return from the system is to have the tasks that are most difficult performed by the physicians with the most experience. I would not object to a resident or intern observing as a board-certified neurologist conducted the examination. I would even probably find satisfaction with one of them conducting parts of the examination, while the seasoned professional was at their side to provide guidance and supervision. I just don't agree with a system that allows the responsibility of detecting damage to the most mysterious and complicated system in the human body, to rest solely upon the judgment and intellect of one of the least experienced doctors in the entire building. And, as my experience proved that day, my intuition was a hundred percent accurate.

According to the young physician who administered my neurological examination, my brain and the rest of my nervous system were all completely healthy. Under normal circumstances, having been given that diagnosis, (and knowing how false it was), would have irritated the hell out of me. But as luck would have it, thanks to the undiagnosed injuries to my frontal lobe, by the time they made their diagnosis official, (a few hours later), I had completely forgotten what my chief complaints were, and so I wasn't able to dispute their findings. So when a well-spoken man in a white coat with a stethoscope around his neck assured me that my mind was in tip-top shape, naturally we took his words to be the absolute truth. And, for reasons I have explained earlier, I could think of no reason to doubt him.

Chapter 6

There is an old sailor's adage known as 'the calm before the storm.' It's used to describe that eerie quiet period of time when the trade winds come to a standstill and the often-chaotic seas go flat as a lake. When I think about the time in my life when I lost my vision for the very first time, I often forget about how wonderful the preceding years were, (understandably so, considering how emotionally traumatic it was to lose my vision). I'm speaking about my high school years. In the grand scheme of things, if the bullying in Elementary school, and going blind after high school graduation represent the two major storms of my childhood, then those years in between, were in a sense the calm before one of my life's major storms, (or the flats described by the riding instructor).

After sailing out of junior high school, (aka middle school), in remarkably better shape than when I entered it, I found myself in the unique situation of being a high school freshman with a boatload of confidence. I owe much of that confidence to my ability to unleash the power of knowledge. There is an old Chinese proverb that goes something like this:

He who asks a question is a fool for a minute. He who does not is a fool forever.

If there was one thing I was really good at, it was asking questions! I discovered that being knowledgeable is more about knowing where to find answers, (and what questions to ask), than it is about the memorization of facts, formulas and theories. My philosophical way of viewing the world caused me to naturally question everything and everyone. One of my teachers once told me how much it concerned her whenever her students did not have any questions to ask after she finished a lecture. Receiving questions and feedback is an educator's quickest way to measure how much of the knowledge was understood and absorbed by the students. For students, (especially poor test takers), it is often the only way to learn and comprehend a complicated subject matter.

Even though I was a good student in high school, I could not come close to matching the grades of those students who were at the very top of my class, however, I refused to let that bother me. Instead, I learned how to run circles around many of them by using many of the street-smart tactics instilled in my brain by the old timers back in my Brooklyn days. For instance, they taught me that you always have a shot at outperforming the competition, (even those who are stronger, faster, more intelligent, or more talented), by outworking, outsmarting and outshining them. This concept is still applicable today for everything from making an impression on a job interview to winning a Super Bowl game. With that in mind, I became well aware that knowing how to obtain and utilize knowledge was far more important, (and powerful), than merely possessing it.

By the time I got to high school, I also realized that gaining and maintaining respect was equally as important as the power of knowledge. It's easy to walk the high school hallways with confidence when you've earned everyone's respect. The key word in that last sentence is earned. Respect doesn't come easily. It is also impossible to fake. My Brooklyn elders taught me that the most genuine way to earn respect is to give it first. Being unselfishly kind and helpful to others commands respect. So does being courteous and polite at all times, regardless of the circumstances. This method of thinking relies upon what is known as ethical reciprocity, (the expectation that people will respond to each other in similar ways). For example, responding with acts of kindness to people who are kind to you. If you think this sounds incredibly familiar to something taught by your religion, then you are a hundred percent correct.

In modern religions we hear it worded in such phrases as: do unto others as you would have them do unto you, as well as love your neighbor as yourself. Jesus Christ loved this way of thinking. So did Confucius and all of their followers, so much so, that it has been named The Golden Rule. The true roots of the Golden Rule are uncertain. It's clear that it was present in the philosophies of ancient Babylon, Egypt, China, India, Persia, Greece, etc. as well as the teachings of all of the world's major religions including Buddhism, Hinduism, Taoism, Zoroastrianism, and of course, Islam, Christianity and Judaism. I think you get the point.

The Golden Rule exists because history has proven that more often than not bad circumstances come to those who treat others poorly, while positive circumstances come to those who treat others well. Some will say it's the will of God while others will tell you that it is the power of Karma. Either way, it's nearly impossible to dismiss this belief of billions of people.

I'm not claiming that every bad circumstance in the future is the consequence of a bad act from the past, although many people will claim that they are. I will tell you that my personal experiences do seem to support this theory, (and certainly do not give me any reason to doubt its validity). Even long before I witnessed it myself, the Golden Rule was introduced to me as a child from so many different sources and in so many ways, that it's nearly impossible for me to pinpoint the exact moment I became a believer. My parents taught it to me, (that I'm certain of). It was also clearly a key component of street-smart survival. I was never a very religious person, but I have always lived my life by the rules of Christianity, (and we all know how important the Golden Rule is to my chosen religion). Even as an American, the equality and justice for all component of our American values, (which is the cornerstone of everything we believe in here in the United States), is predicated on the notion that each of us will treat our fellow citizens with the same respect that we expect them to treat us.

Out of all of my experiences, I can say that these expectations were most exemplified when I was in scouts. The scout slogan is Do a Good Turn Daily. The first six of the twelve points of the scout law highlight specific ways a scout can treat others well: A Scout is Trustworthy, Loyal, Helpful, Friendly, Courteous and Kind. Even in music we were taught the most basic fundamentals of harmony, which fully depends upon every musician in the group unselfishly working together. The more I think about it, the more I realize how much the Golden Rule was imbedded into my mind when I was a child. It is no wonder that I embraced it as a way of life. Heck, I even treated the schoolyard bullies who beat the hell out of me with dignity and respect (if you can imagine such a thing).

By the time I was in high school, all of the positive energy that I had sent out to others in the world eventually started to make its journey back to me, (in a good way, of course). I found that the more I treated others with respect, the more I received it. Like most schools in America, the students in my school were divided into the typical social groups and stereotypes, (try watching the 1985 movie The Breakfast Club to see what I grew up with). Also like most schools in America, there was constant tension and conflicts between the groups. As the social boundaries continued to strengthen, I found myself in the unique situation of being a friend to all of them and an enemy to none. I have no doubt in my mind that this came to be as a result of my constant willingness to build bridges instead of walls. I tried not to judge others, (even those who appeared to be much different). I also benefitted from my desire for diversity. I was probably the only kid in school on the honor roll who played sports, listened to all genres of music, including heavy metal, and who was a member of the marching band, the ski club, a break-dancing crew and a Boy Scout troop. I think all those earlier years of being assaulted for being perceived as being different, led me to unconsciously develop a persona that had something in common with practically everyone. Once again, I cannot help but to make reference to my scouting experience.

Despite what most people assume, Boy Scouts is not just about wearing funny-looking uniforms while learning to be a model citizen or a great outdoorsman. It's also about learning to become a well-rounded individual with an in-depth knowledge of a plethora of skills. For instance, it sparked my interest in a variety of topics like gourmet cooking, small boat sailing and horsemanship, (to name a few). It was also where I learned all about leadership. As I mentioned previously, the core group of friends I made in scouting were the best friends I would ever have. Outside of the confines of our troop meetings and weekend campouts, the members of Troop 398 were from all walks of life. In the troop we were like brothers, (even though many of us would probably have clashed in the real world). After spending a considerable amount of time with a diverse group of people, I learned not only how to relate to the members of the different groups from which they came, but to also truly respect them. With that thought in mind, it is clear that the most important skill I took away from my scouting experience was my people skills.

With the burden of being bullied clearly off my shoulders, I made a promise to never allow myself to let my confidence turn into arrogance. I despise people who are presumptuous. There was no way on earth that I could allow myself to turn into something I hated so dearly. Don't get me wrong, there is nothing wrong with being really good at what you do and rightfully proud of it. I just do not appreciate people who go over the top by displaying too much confidence in a way that is rude and demeaning to others, especially when the confidence is unwarranted, or the way it's displayed is inappropriate. I don't know too many people who find it appealing when another person is conceited and/or obsessed with oneself. Personally, I find it repelling. So with that in mind, I somehow found a way to be full of confidence, without being full of myself.

Despite all this, please don't let me give you the wrong idea about my high school experience. The world still handed me my fair share of teenage turmoil. I still faced the same pressures that most teenagers have to face at one time or another. For instance, (like most other teens), I found myself being betrayed when I let my guard down. This more than likely was the result of me becoming too trustworthy of the wrong individuals. I also had my heart broken pretty badly by the opposite sex on more than one occasion as well. It's funny, even for a kid who felt like he had such an in-depth understanding of the world, I still could be reduced to nothing more than a puppy dog by a pretty girl with the right chemistry. Being a hopeless romantic who wore my heart on my sleeve surely made me vulnerable. It's amazing the effect that love can have on even the strongest of minds. This is true not just for adolescents but also for all ages. All of the pain that was inflicted upon me by the schoolyard bullies... all of their punching and kicking and cruel pranks... none of that could stack up to the pain I felt whenever I had my heart broken. Love is incredible. But when it goes bad it's unbearable.

As a teenager I learned that this is a dilemma that people of all ages face. On one hand we want to open our hearts to allow someone we care for to get close to us. On the other hand, letting that person in leaves us completely vulnerable. As teenagers we quickly learn that the success or failure of personal relationships also relies upon adherence to the golden rule. It's obvious how relationships stand a much better chance of survival in the long-run when both parties treat each other as well as they hope, (or even expect), to be treated. When it comes to love, this is often not a factor in the very beginning of a relationship, because when the right chemistry exists between two people, love will hit them hard like a speeding freight train that'll knock them off of their feet.

For a relationship to move to the next level beyond the initial stop-you-in-your-tracks, heart-throbbing, new love phase, (and into something more permanent), both people involved have to learn to play the game of give and take. For a teenager, this could mean something like being tolerant of the other person's friends or family, in exchange for asking them to do the same for you. For any age it means things like overlooking the other person's flaws in hope that they will return the same kind gesture for you. As you can see, once again the golden rule is the secret to it all.

When I was a teenager I would develop some very deep philosophical thoughts about these kinds of concepts. Then I would take my real-world experiences, (as well as those I observed from others), and I would see which of my theories held true. I would write down, (for future reference), the ones that stood the test of time. One day a good friend came to me for advice on something that he was a little bit shy speaking about. I don't know what made me think of it, but instead of trying to overcome his shyness, I scurried through

101

my piles of loose-leaf paper until I found a passage I had written about the topic he was seeking advice on and let him read it. I still remember that moment clearly, as if it was only yesterday, because I found it overwhelmingly satisfying to witness another person reading my words of wisdom and actually benefiting from them.

I may have still been that skinny geek, but for the first time in my life, I was actually able to unleash a serious dose of power into the world. It was that moment when I discovered for the first time what the English author Edward Bulwer-Lytton meant when he coined the famous saying:

"The pen is mightier than the sword."

Of course, those who are familiar with this saying are aware of how it makes reference to the manner in which written words and communication are more powerful than war and fighting battles. My experience had more to do with the influential edge that written words seemed to have over that which was spoken.

Providing advice aimed at mending an adolescent conflict usually somehow backfires by causing more harm than good. Teenage relationships are often so ridiculously fragile that it takes very little effort to cause a tremendous amount of chaos. Knowing this, it should come as no surprise that it takes ten times the energy, skill, knowledge and time to be the person doing the mending, versus the person who does the destructing.

Considering the complexity involved with even a minor teenage tragedy, (for those who secretly knew about the mending powers of my writings), I quickly became nothing short of an instant hero. In my day there were no cell phones for text messaging, or an internet to transport email or instant messages. With little time to speak to each other between or during classes, we most often communicated the old fashion way (we exchanged notes written with pen and paper that were tightly folded into small paper triangles and conveniently stored in the back pocket of our designer jeans). Just like with texting or electronic messages, writing notes afforded teenagers the opportunity to communicate words that would otherwise be difficult to verbally speak. They also allowed us the opportunity to read the messages at our leisure, (as well as the opportunity to cherish the words by re-reading them over and over again to ourselves or to others).

When I spoke, others didn't really care to listen to what my still changing, high-pitched, cracking voice had to say, however, nobody ever hesitated to take my written words seriously. As a matter of fact, on paper my words were regarded more valuable than the most reputable newspaper advice columnists (because who better to lend advice to teenagers than one of their peers, right?). It still amazes me how I went from the extreme of being an outcast to then becoming an insider.

I still remember the exact moment I became aware, so to speak. I was camping with the scouts at one of our favorite east end parks. It was one of our favorites, because the park's property connected with miles of deserted beach on the Long Island sound. Along most of the shoreline were these tremendous sand bluffs that formed steep cliffs over five hundred feet high. Climbing to the top of one of those bluffs at night was a real treat for the senses. Back in our hometown, we lived too close to the nighttime glow of New York City to view much more than only the very brightest of stars (and eventually everything else was washed out by the big city's light pollution). This was in contrast to the absolutely breathtaking views of the celestial bodies that could be observed out east on a clear night where the skies are much darker.

I remember sitting atop one of those bluffs one sleepless night. I found myself staring at that amazing sky, feeling like I was in a planetarium, and listening to the distant sound of those tiny, but consistent waves crashing below. I remember thinking to myself how time felt like it stood still in such an enchanted place with such an incredible view of the sea below and the universe above. It was then that I started thinking about some real big picture stuff, like how the universe first started, as well as the miracle of life itself. Any scholar will tell you that once you start going down that path, you inevitably start to question the purpose for our existence (aka the meaning of life).

Then you reach this point in the thought process where you start to realize that God must truly exist (because the presence of God provides an explanation to everything that can't be explained). Or you develop an acceptance that our human brains simply do not possess the intellectual power to fully grasp and comprehend the answers (because they are simply so much larger than life and beyond anything we have ever imagined or could ever wrap our brains around). Truth be told, it doesn't really matter what conclusion, (if any) a person takes away from that intellectual journey.

You see, in order to really fully and completely go down that path with your mind, you have to have that rare opportunity where you can completely pause and clear your mind of every other possible thought, (like I did being alone on that bluff that night). And when you do this, you start to gain a sudden and incredible appreciation for how insignificant the daily events of our lives are, (when compared to the overall scheme of things), and how each of us literally have a world of opportunity out there just waiting for us to take control and run with.

The accurate way to describe what happened to me that magical night under the stars is to say that I had an epiphany. If you've often wondered what the heck that term meant when you heard it before, the simplest way I can describe it is that I had a sudden and meaningful realization about something incredibly significant. In my case, I concentrated so hard upon the complexity of solving the meaning of life, that it made me realize how utterly simplistic our day-to-day problems are in comparison. It was like spending time trying to solve the most challenging quantitative physics problem and then being asked to provide guidance and insight on something as elementary as whether or not it is easier to solve a simple addition equation when it is written horizontally or vertically (and then remembering that to many people, the horizontal or vertical dilemma is regarded as a real and respected struggle).

That epiphany changed my life forever, (because once you cross that bridge, there is no turning back). It makes a person realize how we are each the masters of our own destiny. Once you start questioning your very own existence, (as well as that of the universe around you), it puts everything else into perspective. This is why so many people in this world incorporate meditation, yoga and spiritual retreats into their daily lives. These activities allow us the opportunity to awaken our minds and hearts to new horizons. Some people are lucky enough to experience this euphoria while they are alone with their thoughts as they partake in a physical activity like skiing, running, hiking or working out. Others find it necessary to seek an actual pilgrimage to a place they find enchanting enough to allow them the necessary space to fulfill their personal quest for spiritual exploration.

All I know is that whether it takes a simple jog around the neighborhood, or a journey to some remote island in the Pacific, we all owe it to ourselves to seek out our own epiphany. When I had mine, it made me curious as to why it appeared that the majority of the people in this world, (many of them being way more intelligent than myself), will spend their entire lives without ever taking a timeout from the demands of everyday life to do a little soul searching for themselves. It made me realize that for the most part, the vast majority of the people on this earth were living their lives as mere zombies. They were alive, but they really weren't living, (if that makes any sense). The more I thought about this, the more I realized that this was the primary reason why there are so many followers and so few leaders. This was especially true among my fellow high school classmates.

Like the rest of the world, my school was loaded with some incredibly talented individuals. There was surely no shortage of creative minds that emerged from my generation. They were obviously productive and nobody could ever deny that they were overly energetic too. Yet despite all that, the majority of them still went on to continue to live their lives like zombies. They went through all of the motions necessary to live life, (and be successful for the most part). But take a poll and attempt to discover how many of them ever took the time to step aside from their ordinary lives to piece together some extraordinary thoughts, and I guarantee you that you'd be discouraged to learn that very few ever did, or even desired to do so.

Back in High School it amazed me too that this was the case among so many young people. I would have expected it from adults who, (without any fault of their own), find themselves so caught up in the demands of marriage, careers and parenthood, that they don't allow room for much else. But among teenagers with so much time on our hands, and so much useful brain capacity available to process those deeper thoughts... well it was shocking that so few of us possessed the desire to attempt to gain a deeper understanding of life.

When I descended down from that bluff overlooking the beach that night I was a much different and wiser young man than the person I was when I climbed up there a few hours earlier. And when I returned back to my everyday ordinary life, all of my friends were quick to point out that it was pretty darn obvious that I had gained a deeper understanding about life. I didn't really take notice of it myself, until the first time I put on the radio and listened to some popular rock music. For the very first time in my life, I didn't just listen to the music; I actually heard it. I discovered that I now had a profound ability to interpret lyrics and derive emotions from them, even far beyond the original songwriters could have ever dreamed.

Once I started appreciating lyrics, I could not stop. It was as if I had discovered that life had a soundtrack that I never even realized existed. I also discovered that the true measure of whether or not you have the ability to connect with music is whether or not you ever had a song actually cause you to shed some tears. I also learned how much of a motivator the right music could be. I became so obsessed with music that I eventually reached the point where I could feel some songs actually penetrating my soul. I even started writing down some of the meaningful lyrics, because of the great philosophical value I found in them.

I quickly realized that there is a song out there to match every possible mood or human emotion. My intuition told me that there was also something mysterious and powerful about music that I was yet to understand, and it made me feel so wonderful and alive!

Chapter 7

I discovered that life had a soundtrack but nobody told me that the playlist wasn't always going to be what I'd expect it to be. For instance, it could be argued how the song Highway to Hell by AC/DC would have been an appropriate song to have been playing on the radio the moment of my car accident. Instead, *complicated* by Avril Lavigne was the song that was playing right before impact. And now that I think about it, the word complicated turned out to be the most appropriate adjective to label my life after the collision.

My life, (the way it was immediately before the car accident), was in many ways a dream come true. I was kicking ass at work and I had a great relationship with my wife and children.

With success at a great job comes the ability to make more money than you spend. With that ability comes the nice house, the awesome vacations and lots and lots of toys. We were by no means rich like Trump or the Rockefellers, but we were still better off financially in comparison to 90% of the people we met in the world. My ability to wake up every day and go to work as an insurance salesman was by far our greatest asset but all of that changed the moment I was injured in the accident.

The physical injuries to my body obviously took several surgeries and a respectable amount of time to heal. And, yes, I lost some time at work in the interim. However, I soon discovered that healing from my physical injuries was going to be the least of my concerns. It was my less obvious injuries that would, incidentally in the long run, prove to be the most challenging to overcome.

When the doctors gave the green light for me to return to work it didn't take long for me to discover how I had lost my ability to be a successful sales rep. You see, being successful at sales for a large corporation requires a seriously complex blend of skills, intelligence and personality traits. Among other things, it requires extensive product knowledge, sharp communication skills, and a remarkable ability to relate to other people. Many people go through all of the motions yet still easily fail. Not only does it take a unique type of individual to excel in sales, it also takes one who is almost completely self-motivating who also has a keen sense of time management and broad enough shoulders to overcome constant rejection. Many sales positions, (like mine), have the potential to be rewarding with an almost unlimited amount of commission, (at the sacrifice of not having much of a base salary, if any).

As one of the elite sales reps in my field, I accepted the fact that I had chosen one of the most difficult career paths, in exchange for the potential to earn the big bucks. I lived by the philosophy that was best quoted by Tom Hanks when he played the role of Jimmy Dugan in the 1992 movie A League of Their Own:

"It's supposed to be hard. If it wasn't hard, everyone would do it. The hard is what makes it great."

The problem I discovered when I returned to work full-time after my car accident, was that that for the first time in my career I found the job to actually be too hard for me. This fact, however, made absolutely no sense to me, or anyone who knew me. It was as if I became one of those hapless souls who had no business attempting to go through the motions, because they will simply never succeed in the business. The oddest thing about my new inability to succeed was that it was impossible to pinpoint the exact reason why. I was like a professional baseball player in a major hitting slump. I was working my ass off doing everything right, yet at the end of the day I had nothing to show for it except a bunch of almosts and what-ifs. The closest thing to a valid explanation that I could come up with to describe what was wrong with me was that I had somehow lost my mojo, (yes, I know it sounds really out-there to say that Joe lost his mojo, but it's true).

The more serious problem was that when you don't come from money and you are raising a family that has an expensive lifestyle with a nice house, cars, boats, and other toys that go along with it, (as well as a full schedule of expensive hobbies yourself), you find yourself with some serious monthly expenses. Someone once explained to me how it is human nature for us to elevate our lifestyles to match our income levels. As wise as it is to be frugal, reality is that we all feel that because life is so short, we should enjoy what we are able to enjoy while we have the ability to enjoy it. The American way of life has evolved into this new reality, and I was no exception to this theory.

Many experts will argue how spending money, (versus saving it), is good for the economy. Of course, accountants and financial advisors will warn against it. The truth of the matter is that here in America, even living above one's current means, (by using credit), isn't the worse thing in the world to do so long as your income continues to rise in the future and you aren't faced with any sort of personal catastrophes. In my case, I was hit with both at the same time. Being out on disability leave from my job several times over the year that followed my car accident left me with a mountain of medical bills that were in excess of my health insurance benefits. Also, my refusal to let my family sacrifice and give up anything while I was out on disability, meant that I had no other choice other than to rely upon credit cards to help pay our expenses.

Upon returning to work, I fully expected to go through a short transition period before I would be able to get back up to full speed. What I did not expect was the discovery that I had lost my mojo. Initially I didn't let it bother me; I just assumed that I was rusty and out of practice.

But as more time passed, the more I would realize that my inability to sustain any meaningful level of production rested solely upon my shoulders. For the very first time in my career, my incredibly successful job actually felt difficult to me. What made it even worse was the fact that I knew that something was wrong with me or different about me and I simply didn't have a clue what the heck it was. It's tough to actually put into words how frustrating this was for me. The problem with this particular type of frustration

112

is that it easily evolves into depression. When depression sets in, (especially for an overachiever), it turns an otherwise bearable slump into an actual rut.

The significant difference between a slump and a rut, in my opinion, is the attitude, outlook and approach of the person going through it. A slump can be incredibly depressing, however, no matter how depressing a slump may be, it is still conquerable, (and can end at any moment), so long as the person going through the slump doesn't lose their sense of urgency and desire to succeed. On the other hand, when a person is in a rut, they lose that desire or sense of urgency and simply stops caring. Ruts are so much more difficult to snap out of, because before a person can start to succeed again, they have to actually believe that they have the ability to succeed in the first place. Looking back on that dark period, it's obvious to me that I was in a serious rut, because I realized that I not only lost my mojo, but also lost my confidence and I didn't even seem to care about losing either. My income dropped almost in half as a result of my poor sales results and I wasn't even slightly motivated to do anything about it. Being that person who under ordinary circumstances is that extraordinary optimist that I described earlier, I never fair very well when my spirit is broken. It was so out of character for me, because it started to seem like the only thing I was good at was making excuses. What a hypocrite I was becoming! I transformed into the exact type of individual that I so often despised, and it didn't even phase me.

I wish I could say that this was the first time that this had happened to me. Truth be told, there was an earlier period in my life when I also found myself in a very dark place. I'm making reference to the period of time when I lost my vision. I was only eighteen years old when my vision started to rapidly disappear. It started with the need for thicker, more powerful prescription glasses. Less than a month later I was trading those glasses in for an even thicker pair. This went on a few more times until the optometrist declared that my vision had deteriorated so much that I had reached the threshold of what eyeglasses were physically capable of correcting. I was given no choice but to graduate to contact lenses.

Without corrective lenses, my vision loss advanced to the point where the only line I could read on the eye chart out of either eye was the top one with the giant E (and even that was blurry). There are no words to describe how pathetic this made me feel. I mean seriously, not being able to read anything but the giant capital E on the top of an eye test chart? I didn't realize it at the time, but the emotions that I would feel decades later when I discovered that I lost my mojo after my car accident, were strikingly similar to the way I felt when I was discovering how I was rapidly losing my vision.

The strange thing was that the eye doctor didn't seem too concerned with diagnosing the reason for my rapid loss of eyesight. I guess he felt that there was no cause for alarm as long as he could continue to correct my vision using contact lenses. The only problem was that shortly after my vision loss exceeded the outer limits of what eyeglasses could handle, it also rapidly surpassed what his expertise could handle too.

Ask any physician to speak candidly about how it feels when this happens to them, and I guarantee they will tell you how the section of their Hippocratic Oath that addresses how they should not be ashamed to say "I know not" is a mental struggle that is not easy to accept. On one hand, they want to stay true to the oath because it's supposed to be what is best for the patient. On the other hand, there is a whole array of reasons for them to feel that handing off a case that is too complicated is like conceding and waving a surrender flag (and that could very likely do some serious damage to their elite image and personal ego).

In my case, I went through hell trying to be fitted for soft contact lenses. It was the summer of our high school graduation, and most of my fellow graduates were having the time of their lives celebrating. Not me. I spent almost the entire two months being passed from one doctor to the next, as each one failed to craft lenses that could fit my eyes properly. This made me feel like some kind of freak science experiment. Apparently, instead of being perfectly round and smooth, the surface of my corneas had rapidly grown cone-shaped and irregular. They called this condition, astigmatism. I called it a pain in my ass. The astigmatism was causing my vision to go out of whack. It also made it tough for contact lenses to fit comfortably on the surface of my corneas without slipping, folding or popping out.

I desperately needed to see well again (and in a hurry), because I was counting down the days to my first day of college. The plan was for me to live at home and drive myself to and from the university each day and to work in the evenings. But as that countdown started to wind down, and summertime progressed, it started to feel very likely that I would have to forfeit my academic scholarship and postpone my college enrollment. You see, even if I managed to somehow secure and finance last-minute living arrangements on campus, I still had the unresolved problem of not being able to yet read or write without assistance.

That was the year 1985. Back then we didn't have the laws that exist today that protect people with disabilities. Back then we had special schools for the blind and almost blind, because mainstream schools were not equipped, (nor required), to accommodate the visually impaired. A quick call to the dean of students confirmed that my new college was not obligated, (nor willing), to make any special arrangements to provide me with assistance. Even if I solved the mobility problem by having someone guide me around campus, I still would have no way to prepare for and take tests, write term papers or fulfill most of the other academic requirements.

Lucky for me, this is when those very special rigid gas permeable, (R.G.P.), lenses came into my life. Unlike soft contacts, the R.G.P.s held their shape and basically created a new perfectly round artificial surface to compensate for my irregular cone-shaped corneas. Add in the proper magnification, and the R.G.P.s allowed me to once again obtain 20/20 vision, despite my severe astigmatism.

The first time a doctor popped in a pair of those R.G.P. lenses into my eyes, the correction of my vision was so dramatic that it actually made my head feel like it was spinning. Those tiny plastic semi spheres were a modern marvel; a miracle advance in medicine. These new magic lenses did not, however, provide a cure for, (or slow down), my rapid loss of vision. In the grand scheme of things they were simply an optical tool, much like visual crutches.

While out on the open sea, every sailor is familiar with the false sense of hope that is felt while sailing through the eye of a storm. After being beaten and battered by the first part of the storm, the calm seas in the storm's eye are a welcome refuge. The sunny skies and mild weather are so mesmerizing that the sailors practically forget about the surrounding storm and how they still have the entire second half of it to endure. That is exactly how I felt when I first started wearing R.G.P.s. They provided a much-needed temporary fix to my vision loss.

The emphasis in that last sentence should be on the word temporary. I say this because soon after, as I was celebrating my reunion with the visually acute world, (and once again living a semi-normal life), my eyes then began to develop what can only be described as severe visual disturbances.

It all started with double vision. In my case I was seeing separate and distinct double vision out of each eye, so that when I focused on an object like the moon with both of my eyes, the image being projected to my brain contained FOUR moons scattered in a circle. At the same time I had another new development; my new R.G.P. contact lenses started popping out of my eyes because they no longer fit properly. I think when this started to happen, I started to make the transition back then from slump to rut.

These newly developed complications made me an even more frequent visitor to eye doctors. At one point I was visiting multiple specialists on a weekly basis. The assortment of examination equipment used by those eye doctors to evaluate the eyes and vision is astonishing.

Their workstation reminded me of a Swiss Army Knife, the way all of those gizmos and gadgets swing out of that central worktable. One of the most intriguing devices is known as a keratometer. The device is used to measure the curvature of the cornea to determine the degree of astigmatism. To put that in layman's terms, it's a tool that can measure how steep the cone of a cornea is. Nowadays the complete topography of the cornea can be mapped out by an electronic device with the help of a computer. But before technology simplified our lives, eye doctors had to do everything by hand.

To calculate measurements using the keratometer, the eye doctor would have the patient look inside the barrel of the machine as it projected numerous rings of light on the surface of the cornea. Looking into the device was like looking down a long endless black tunnel that was illuminated by brightly lit rings every few feet. It was a tasty visual treat, even for the visually impaired.

In the early stages of my disease, any doctor could simply turn some dials and within seconds be able to record the measurements of my corneas. But as my disease progressed, the curvature of my corneas grew so steep that they were beyond what a keratometer was able to measure. Once again my condition exceeded the limitations of science, (and once again the local eye doctors could not explain why).

The severe steep cone shape of my corneas explained why I started losing so many contact lenses. Instead of resting on my corneas around their outside rims, my contacts started riding on the peaks of my sharply pointed corneas like see-saws. All it took was a slight breeze, a few blinks, or a quick turn of my head to send one or both of my lenses flying toward the floor. The only solution to that problem was to fit me with tiny R.G.P. lenses that could sit on the small diameters of the peaks of my corneas. Since no device was capable at that time of measuring the actual contour of my corneas, the only way to find a good fit was to keep trying various size lenses in my eyes until we found a size that fit comfortably. This may sound simple enough, but it was actually a very long and tedious task.

It was not easy getting used to those long eye examinations. Assuming the role of the patient with the mysterious symptoms was one of toughest transitions I ever had to go through in my life. I have to say, I found it to be incredibly frustrating. I felt the same way later in life when I lost my mojo. In both situations, I was well aware of what I had before I lost it. When it came to losing my ability to earn a decent living, you need to understand how I reached the level where I was at, prior to losing it to understand how it was equally as devastating as losing my eyesight.

You see, after moving from Brooklyn to Long Island, both of my parents went on to become hard working small business owners. In the world I knew, every single day was a hustle. If you didn't work hard, you didn't make any money. If you wanted to make more money, you simply worked harder. In that world nothing happened unless you made it happen. The only thing more important than working your ass off, was keeping customers happy so that they would hopefully refer more customers to you, (so you could in turn make more money).

With those attributes being instilled in me, (thanks to my parents), it was another reason why it became natural for me to pursue a career in sales, where the harder I work, the more money I can make. The best part about it is that feeling at the end of the day, when I would be so exhausted, yet felt incredibly satisfied to know that I had worked my ass off.

Back in the day when dad and I were fishing together every weekend, we were invited to join a local fishing club. It was a great opportunity to meet and become friends with other islanders who shared our passion for the sea. The club sponsored weekend fishing tournaments for its members. Among the members of this club, was this nice fellow who consistently placed in the money by weighing-in some very impressive size fish in almost every weekend contest. When we got to know him a little better, we learned that he was the first to admit that he was far from being a very skilled angler.

When I asked the fisherman what the secret to his success was, (if it wasn't angling skill), he did not hesitate to tell me how he had an edge over most of the other members of the club, because he was able to get out and fish during the week, while everyone else had to work. By the time each weekend contest started, he already knew where in the bay the fish would most likely be concentrated, and what type of bait or lures they were most interested in biting. The other anglers would spend a good part of the weekend tournament trying to figure out this formula, while this guy would always be one step ahead of them.

I could tell that the man was in his mid-to-late forties, (too young to be retired). My only assumption was that he was so wealthy, that he was able to retire at an unusually early age. I later found out that he wasn't retired, nor was he super wealthy. He merely worked like crazy from

November until April, without taking a single vacation day. He saved all of his days, so during the fishing season he could take off whenever he wanted to. It occurred to me that this man was simply being rewarded in the summer for the sacrifices he made during the winter.

Very early on in my career I bought into this philosophy and made it my own:

Live your life today like nobody else wants to live, so that someday you can live your life like nobody else can.

I made my first attempt at mimicking that fisherman's way of life was when I was a sophomore in college. I made the decision to take as many night classes as possible, so I could work almost full-time during the day. Instead of going away and living in a dorm at some party school, I chose to stay at home and commute to a boring technical college. I found this to be incredibly rewarding. It proved to be just what a runt of the litter like me needed so I continued it throughout my remaining college years. I spent the spring and fall semesters living like none of my peers would ever dream of living. But come the Winter and Summer breaks, I was the one with the awesome new sports car, nice clothes and a wad of money in my pocket, while the rest of them were counting quarters and dimes to try to come up with enough change to order a slice of pizza. I was living the life that they could only dream about.

This was my first taste of what it felt like to earn enough money to be financially independent. It was also the first time in my life where even the arrogant bullies envied me.

When we graduated college, my peers, who spent four to six years away at college partying found it extremely challenging to land decent jobs without any prior work experience.

Meanwhile, I had a new position waiting for me at one of the largest financial institutions in the world months before graduation.

When my career really started to take off, I took that sacrifice today/prosper tomorrow philosophy to the next level. I realized that if it worked on a seasonal scale then it would work even better in the long-term, big picture scheme of things. So, as a young and energetic new sales person, I worked some seriously crazy hours. I remember not taking more than a few vacation days for over a five-year period. I worked much harder than anyone around me was willing to work, with the thinking that this would allow me to someday rest and take it easy more than anyone else could hope to. When I was single, (as well as during the earlier years that we were married, and when the children were still very young), the timing was perfect to make those kinds of sacrifices.

All of those hours I spent prospecting and selling, gave me a ton of practice dealing with people. I started to realize that most people despised salesmen, because of how pushy they could be. I also realized how people didn't want someone to push products on them. Instead, they desired someone to help them make educated buying decisions. With this realization very early on in my career, I adopted the consultative approach to sales. It can be argued that I became a very successful salesperson by being an anti-salesperson.

I also learned how much easier my job was when I slowed down enough to get to know my customers and to let my customers get to know me. Once I started to relate to them and make real emotional connections, the sales started to fly in. I honed those skills... perfecting them to the point where they became second nature to me. Eventually those skills reached a new level that even I didn't fully understand. It was if they became some sort of magical powers or special gift. This, my friend, was the very birth of that mysterious entity that I refer to as my mojo.

And thanks to all of that crazy hustling, (in combination with my mojo), we were able to own and maintain a nice house in a nice neighborhood with a beautiful water view. And while my town is really nice, it's by no means one of the Island's wealthiest. New York, (and more specifically, Long Island), is arguably the most expensive place to raise a family in the United States. What Frank Sinatra said about New York is true; if a person can make it here, they can make it anywhere. Like most family guys in my shoes here in Long Island, most of what we put into our bank accounts goes right back out to pay expenses. That's why my greatest financial asset became my ability to wake up each day and go to work, (being alive and healthy). My second greatest financial asset was my relentless desire to succeed.

I know this sounds strange, but when I tried to get back into the swing of things after the accident, and found that I could not succeed, it actually felt as if I had damaged the part of my brain that stored my ability to excel at my job. Absurd as it sounds, I believed this was true.

When my brains were getting rattled around in my head I didn't have a clue what was being damaged. However, as

I mentioned, once I tried to apply myself it was so obvious that my mind now contained a giant void where it once housed (among other things), my ability to relate to my clients.

As you can imagine, losing my mojo was as devastating to me as losing my vision. In both circumstances I was losing both my ability to connect with the world, because one of my most valuable modes of perception was distorted. I was like a ship that was losing my compass just as a thick fog was rolling in. I found myself completely blindsided, (no pun intended). The timing seemed so disturbingly unfair. I could actually not imagine a more inappropriate time for tragedy to strike in my life, than at such crucial moments, when things finally started to go my way.

I have to tell you, witnessing my conscience reach the point where it shunned off every whisper of hope in favor of a dark, gloomy outlook was a terrifying experience. To have it happen to me twice... well that was simply horrific. There is a famous quote by the German philosopher Friedrich Nietzsche from the late 1800s that says:

"What doesn't kill us, makes us stronger."

This theory suggests that the strengths of the dynamic individuals who you and I are today, are the sums of all of the experiences we've survived (the good, the bad, and the ugly included). As you are about to discover, there were moments during each of my ordeals where the survival of my sanity was questionable. But thanks to some perfectly timed miracles (and my strong desire to be triumphant) I was able to emerge victoriously from my battles with darkness. I even managed to learn a thing or two about myself (and life) along the way.

Chapter 8

In order to fully appreciate the implications of losing my mojo and my amazing journey to regain it, you first need a closer look at my journey into blindness when I was younger. Over the years I somehow suppressed the entire experience of losing my eyesight and the cornea transplants that helped me regain it, (as well as the emotions that went along with those experiences). Thanks to the modern marvels of the medical field, my vision has since been stable enough to allow me to experience numerous long stretches of time where I've actually (even though it was temporary) forgotten that I was any different than the guy standing next to me. But, don't forget I'm a big fan of the out-of-sight/out-of-mind mentality when it comes to processing and storing bad memories from the past. So in order to truly convey to you what it actually feels like to lose your vision, it actually takes an incredible amount of effort on my part to stir up feelings that should otherwise be best left undisturbed.

Taking you with me to such a dark and unforgiving place in my mind, (where I keep those memories under lock and key), is so uncharacteristic for such an optimistic person like me to do. It is said that in the world of good and evil, (or Yin and Yang), everything must balance out evenly. So for every positive in the world, there must be a negative force of equal weight. For all of you Star Wars movie fans out there, this is the equivalent to how there must always be a balance in The Force at all times. In my religion there is a Hell run by The Devil, just as there is a Heaven that is run by God. If you accept these beliefs to be true, then you also must accept that in order for each of us to have positive attributes we must also have equally as strong dark sides. Some of us display what-you-see-is-what-you-get personalities, while many of us hide our skeletons in a closet.

In my case, I know it may not be considered the healthiest thing to do, but I bury my unbearable dark-side, so the world only gets to see the parts of me that shine the brightest. Truth be told, I am at peace living this way. Every time I size up the challenges that a new day brings, I am well aware of the fact that I deprive the strength that is required to overcome those new obstacles from the secret darkness I carry around inside me. I believe that our sorrow actually adds depth to our personas. Without them, we would be shallow, simple-minded, and certainly not inspirational. Want proof? Simply take a look at the darkest, most trying eras of mankind and you will discover how each of those periods also produced some of the most significant works of art, music and literature, as well as some of the most amazing advances in science and technology.

The problem with sorrow and personal pain is that it often leads an individual into a state of depression. The why me syndrome is all too natural for us to feel whenever we find ourselves faced with grief that we do not believe we deserve. The first time I lost my eyesight is a classic example of this.

One would think that after having to endure all of that undeserved hardship bestowed upon me by the schoolyard bullies, I would have been spared from any additional major grief, (at least for a while) because it could be argued that I had already been given my fair share. Well, the first rule about grief that we all must accept is that there are no rules!

In the overall scheme of things there is no valid argument for feeling that my blindness was not deserved, because the reality is that it didn't matter one bit whether or not my childhood was plagued with turmoil. Likewise, I was not stricken with blindness as a punishment for any of my prior actions. It's easy for me now to reflect back on that period of time and make these statements today, however, back in the day when it was all happening to me, (and so quickly I might add), I found myself spending many sleepless nights attempting to decipher the answer to the question, why me?

Our quest for answers from the medical field about my eye condition reached a critical level of urgency shortly after I started my first semester of college. My initial emotional reaction to my eye problems was that of complete and utter embarrassment. It felt much along the same lines as what it felt like being bullied when I was younger, (only this time it was life itself that was doing the bullying and not my peers). As always, all I wanted to do was to play it cool, so as not to draw any more attention to myself. Life as a freshman in college was hard enough. The extra anxiety I had to carry around all of the time was more than enough to put me over the edge, (as I'm about to explain).

One thing about hard contact lenses that makes them much less versatile than the modern soft contact lenses that are most common today, is that they cannot be worn while sleeping. That means that every night before I go to sleep I have to go into the bathroom and remove my contact lenses. My mom used to say that I had to take my eyes out before I went to bed. I can still hear the words she would yell down to my room and say, "Joey did you remember to take your eyes out?" As funny as this may sound, there was more truth in her analogy than you will ever know. Even to this day, the moment I remove my contact lenses, my vision instantly reverts back to a distorted mess of confusing halos, streaking lights and multiple indescribable images. Some of the images float across my field of vision, while others actually pulsate with every beat of my heart.

Wearing contact lenses is much like wearing a mask that allows me to pretend to be normal like everyone else. Removing my contact lenses at the end of every day is a constant reminder of my true pathetic reality. For a stressed-out college freshman, this was a tough nut to swallow. Sleeping became an outlet to help me escape from that new reality. It got to the point where I didn't even mind horrible nightmares, (you know you are heading down a dark path when you prefer a night of sick nightmares over your own real life).

The problem I had was that I knew what it was like to be able to wake up every morning and immediately focus my vision upon the world around me. I had known that for my entire life. Vision is one of those remarkable gifts we often take for granted because we are born with it.

You can't blame us for regarding vision as an absolute necessity. So I think you can appreciate how devastating it must have been to have my vision taken away from me at the tender age of nineteen. The medical world's lack of answers on how to get my vision back simply compounded that awful feeling.

At first I tried to make the best of the situation, but even for a super optimist, this sort of burden starts to take its toll on your psyche rather quickly. So instead of starting each new day with a bright outlook, (as I had prior to grown accustomed to my entire life), I would open my eyes and become immediately discouraged by what I saw, (and the lack of what I could see).

Then I had to go through the annoying ritual of disinfecting the lenses, rinsing them, and placing them precisely on my corneas without dropping them, (or any of the other dozen or so things that could go wrong while handling them).

Placing contact lenses on my eyes is like a mad intensive rush for my brain as my vision goes from complete distortion to a bright crisp picture. I can actually feel the shock travel from my retinas through the optic nerve, all the way to the visual cortex in the back of my brain. It's a really sick sensation. Just imagine instantly going from viewing the world through a cloudy, distorted broken pair of dirty sunglasses to instantly seeing it in crisp super high definition. It's easy for me to explain this now to others because anyone in the modern world today can understand and appreciate what it means to view something in high definition. But back in the mid-1980s, there simply was nothing in the world to compare or relate this to. When I tell this story, many people at this point say to me the words big deal. And you know what? If that's all I had to deal with then I would say they are correct. Dealing with the inconvenience of waking up blind as a bat, but then being able to obtain perfect vision after popping in some contact lenses is not the end of the world. However, this was still all part of the calm before the storm.

As any college student will tell you, a full-time curriculum demands a great deal of hours to successfully complete the course requirements. My classes started shortly after 8am. Living thirty minutes from campus, and needing enough time to account for traffic, finding parking and walking across campus, meant that I had to leave my house by 7am every morning to get to class on time. I also did not get out of work until 9:30pm every night. This translated into seventeen or eighteen-hour days by the time I got home, unwound and went to bed, (and that's not even counting the nights where I had to stay up super late to write term papers or cram for exams).

The problem was that my contact lenses were really only meant to be worn no more than a maximum of eight to ten hours per day. I wanted so much to be normal that I continued to live my life just as foolishly as any other eighteen-year-old would. This meant taking risks and constantly living on the edge. Needless to say, I ignored the eight-to-ten-hour rule, because it simply wasn't feasible with my demanding schedule and lifestyle. What nobody happened to have told me, (mostly because my eye disorder was still undiagnosed), was that as the cones of my corneas continued to steepen, (as the severity of my astigmatism progressed), the corneas themselves started to thin. As this condition worsened, my corneas started to become severely scarred. Excessively wearing hard contact lenses on those thinning corneas only compounded that situation. This in turn caused me to experience sensitivity to light. For the first time during my battle with Keratoconus, I felt ocular pain, (and let me tell you, it hurt like a son-of-a-bitch).

Experiencing the raw sensation of pain is often a wakeup call. For me, it brought into perspective for the first time how severe my condition actually was. Up until that point I didn't have one ounce of hope for a positive ending, (because no doctor on the island had been able to give me an accurate diagnosis). As bad as that sounds, it didn't feel like it was a critical situation, thanks to the false hope that was created by the nice vision I had been able to achieve by wearing contact lenses. But false hope is as deceptive to our conscious mind as a clever magic trick. And when the illusion created by smoke and mirrors wears off, all you are left with is a solid dose of reality. For me, that meant discovering how it was becoming evident that all hope would soon be lost. My vision was rapidly disappearing and there wasn't a damn thing I could do about it, (and that just plain sucked!!!).

It was pretty obvious too that I was entering the final devastating stage of vision loss. This horrible information was a burden that I carried around without telling another soul. Yes, the right thing to do should have been to immediately inform my parents, however, I could see the frustration, (that comes with the lack of hope), taking its toll on them both emotionally and financially. Instead, I made every attempt to conceal the shocking ordeal the best that I

132

could. If you think it would be a simple task to conceal being blind as a bat, you'd better think again.

No matter what anyone says, out of the five senses, vision is by far the one that provides the brain with the greatest awareness of the world around us. It's easy to understand how, (and why) we become so dependent upon our eyesight. I mean let's face it; we do live in a visual world. Inserting my contact lenses in the morning used to be my salvation because of how they improved my vision so much, that I practically forgot that I had an eye problem. But those newly developed scars on my corneas started to block my vision, so much so, that even with the contact lenses in my eyes, seeing clearly was now a struggle. To make matters even worse, my corneas grew so steep that even the smallest lenses no longer fit properly. Just keeping the lenses in my eyes was a chore in itself.

I don't know which was more difficult to hide; the fact that my vision loss had progressed to the point of near uselessness or the emotional trauma that the experience created. I tried so hard to keep it together. I was certain that informing my parents would have only led to yet another disappointing eye doctor appointment. Only this time it would have been the mother of all disappointments, because it was clear to me that the news would have been that I was practically legally blind. I was no fool. I was well aware of my condition. Informing the world was no different than surrendering, and I simply was not ready to concede. So even though it was a foolish thing to do, (as well as an incredibly risky one), I carried on with my life by doing my best to pretend that nothing was wrong. This included driving to and from school and work.

What an idiot I was putting both others and myself on the road at risk every time I squinted my way around behind the wheel of my car. So much for being that super responsible Eagle Scout everyone thought I was. I wonder how many parts of the scout law I broke during that troubled period in my life. That's what FEAR will do to a person. It can literally cause temporary personality changes. In my case, I lost my grip on reason. My keen sense of judgment was gone. The careless driving was only the start of it. By the time I arrived at school, I was so mentally exhausted from the drive, that after parking my car I would often hop into the back seat to lie down and take a catnap, in hope of regaining enough energy to make it through the rest of the day.

The first few times the catnaps worked. They may have caused me to arrive late to my classes, but at least I still was able to attend. As driving became more of a burden, the required length of the naps increased. This inevitably led to having to skip my morning classes altogether. A week after midterms, driving on highways became far too burdensome. I could still manage to get around by driving on slower moving side streets, however, this meant that in order to get to work on time, I had to skip out on my last afternoon classes as well.

Slowly and steadily my world was collapsing around me. The only thing that distracted me from the incredible stress of losing my vision was the even larger stress of knowing that I was jeopardizing my scholarship, (and most likely blowing my entire future). The pressure reached the point where it was simply unbearable. I sought the stress relief provided by nicotine through the nasty habit of cigarette smoking. When it was clear that smoking alone was not strong enough, I then turned to drinking alcohol. It's amazing how the evil vices of the world are waiting in the shadows whenever one's own reality becomes too much of a burden to handle.

I started to convince myself that I had spent my entire life pretending that I was normal, when in fact the bullies seem to have had it right all along; I was indeed a freak. So instead of sitting inside one of the lecture halls, classrooms or labs, (among all of the normal people on campus and preparing myself for a respectable future), I found myself exiled to the commuter parking lot on the far side of campus, where a freak like me could drink myself into oblivion in total isolation. I wasn't suicidal or anything, I just felt like the world didn't need to be burdened by such a pathetic loser and his stupid eye problems. Low self-esteem and/or self-pity were never my cup of tea (even though you'd think they would have been at some point in my childhood considering all that I had experienced). So needless to say, that state of mind being all new to me was not something I was prepared for.

Isolation, (on the other hand), was right up my alley. I actually did have a steady girlfriend at the time, that I was pretty serious about for a few years leading up to this point, but she was smart enough to bail on me at the precise moment that my disease caused me to become high maintenance, (precisely when I needed her companionship the most). She broke it off with a bang too by leaving me for her best friend's boyfriend. They did it right under my nose too. We were at the mall on a double date, getting some pizza and going to see a movie. The girls had to use the ladies' room, so the other guy and I walked over to purchase the movie tickets.

Incidentally at this point, I was down to only being able to wear one contact lens in one eye.

Guys and girls are so different. When two girls who just met each other are alone for the first time they tend to be either extremely friendly or extremely shy. When it comes to two guys who just met, it usually is a battle of egos to determine which of the two is perceived to be the coolest. Maybe it's a New York/New Jersey macho guy thing that causes us to put on a tough guy image when out on the town with others and our dates, (or maybe teenagers everywhere do the same). All I know is that evening my ego took a solid hit square on the chin. You see, on our way back across the mall to meet up with girls, my one and only contact lens popped out of my eye, leaving me completely blind. I had no choice but to crawl around on the floor to search for the tiny lens by hand. I lost all of my dignity and respect as crowds of people walked by staring at the helpless image of me grasping around for my lens on the filthy ground.

There still remains some debate over the motive behind what happened next. As I was searching the area where I suspected my contact lens had most likely come to rest on the floor, I heard the crackling sound of the lens being crushed under that other guy's shoe. Some people have argued that it was purely accidental. Personally, I think it was an intentional act of pure evil. I am confident of this because I eventually found out that he and my girlfriend had already been secretly fooling around with each other for several weeks, prior to that evening. Unaware of their secret love affair, (and not wanting to ruin anyone's night), I foolishly agreed to still go to the movie, despite being able to only hear and not actually watch it. Knowing how I was unable to focus upon anything that was more than a half-inch away from my eyes, my sinister ex-girlfriend took advantage of the opportunity by holding hands with her secret lover while I sat there right beside them (and I truly did not have a clue!). I came to find this out after the fact, which I guess was somewhat of a good thing.

There is an ever-popular saying of unknown origin:

"When it rains, it pours."

Whoever the genius was who scripted those words, surely was referring to the phenomenon that describes how bad events seem to hit us all at once when we are already down on our luck. As someone who normally is that pure optimist, I can't say that I ever had any motivation to explore the validity of this claim or its possible causes. When life is victimizing a person with a string of horrible events with unusual frequency, the last thing that person wants to, (or needs to do), is analyze their situation. Until you become so overly depressed about it that you no longer give a shit, (and that does happen), your survival instincts will dictate that you concentrate all of your efforts upon implementing the quickest solutions to the problems at hand.

The fact that I was caught completely off-guard by the failure of the relationship with that steady girlfriend taught me a valuable lesson on the limitations of my philosophical insights. That lesson was that no matter how great I was at helping other people sort out their problems, it was clearly evident that I had zero ability to help myself. I may have been ahead of my time in comparison to my peers when it came to philosophical wisdom, but that did not mean that I would be immune to the trials and tribulations that were part of growing up. Somewhere out there I'm sure there is a famous quote in existence that would be quite appropriate right now to summarize how it is possible to be really good at providing equitable solutions for the problems of others, while remaining totally clueless about one's own troubles. I guess I must have missed that lesson when the elders taught it back in my Brooklyn days!

Not a single person from Brooklyn, or anywhere else, had ever informed me that even the best therapists in the world still need to seek the professional assistance of other therapists to help them remain mentally healthy. Out of all of the times in my life when I would have my heart broken, this particular time will always stand out at as being the one that hit me the hardest. In the long run it wasn't so much about losing the girl as it was about the discovery that I failed to see it coming, (and lacked the power to fix it). Up until that point in time I regarded myself as being a relationship guru. This image was based upon the positive feedback I received from my peers who constantly benefited from my advice.

Not being able to benefit from my own advice meant that I had no distinct advantage when it came to making relationships work. The problem was that I made the crucial error of assuming that I did. So at the time in my life when my world was closing in from almost every possible direction, I was certain that my strong will and confidence would be powerful enough to get me through it all.

Discovering that I was a failure at my own relationship was a mighty blow that came at the time in my life when I was most vulnerable. It was a knockout punch, so devastating that it shattered my confidence into tiny pieces. I was approaching my darkest hour, both literally and figuratively speaking. The very last thing I needed at that point was to have my lights punched out prematurely by a sucker punch from the person who I trusted the most.

It was all over for me at that point. As far as I was concerned, I had crossed over the, I don't give a shit line, and there was no turning back. I stopped taking phone calls from friends. I stopped meeting up with them in clubs. No more malls, no more movies, no more bowling, no more hanging out at billiard halls. I even gave up fishing with my dad on the weekends. As far as I was concerned, life was no longer worth living. I was going blind and there was nothing anyone could do to stop it. I second-guessed every word of advice that I had ever given. I stopped going to my college classes, because I saw no point in obtaining a degree. I called in sick to work as often as they would allow. When I did show up to work I began to allow shoplifters to walk out the door with stolen merchandise. I put in such little effort at work, that I would actually charge ridiculously low prices when ringing up any items that weren't properly labeled with a price tag, (instead of leaving the register to search for the correct price).

I let hundreds, (maybe even thousands), of dollars walk out the door and I just did not care. When some of my coworkers hinted that they wanted to sneak a few bucks from the cash register when the boss wasn't looking, I didn't hesitate to stand in front of the surveillance camera to block the view as they did their dirty little deed. Looking back on those actions, I can safely say that I must have been subconsciously on a suicide mission to get my ass fired. I mean, seriously, I did all of those things, all the while being well aware that the owner of the store required every employee to undergo mandatory polygraph tests every few months. Needless to say, I was given a pink slip and I really didn't care about that either. As a matter of fact, I think it pleased me to know that I finally rid myself of my last formal obligation. As obscure as this sounds, (coming from me of all people), the acknowledgement that I didn't have any more reasons to get out of bed in the morning, actually brought the first smile to my face in months.

As my self-esteem spiraled into that dark wicked pit, my selection of music changed too. I found myself constantly replaying Pink Floyd's The Wall album over and over again. I started to become extremely lethargic too. The soundtrack of my life became that of a mad bugger who lost his ability to deal with reality, so he builds a mental wall for isolation and protection from the cruel world around him. In the movie, the main character named, Pink, was a child protected by a mom who grows up to be betrayed by a woman. He is worshiped by many, yet is unable to provide any salvation for himself other than his ability to completely shut out the world, (including those who really care about him). This might as well have been the story of my life. I can recite for you from memory the lyrics to every song in that two-album set. I know the timing of every drumbeat, the key of every guitar chord, and the precise moment of every sound effect. When I wasn't listening to the music on the record player, I would watch the movie on the television set in my room with my stereo hard-wired to it, (no such thing as home theater systems or surround sound back in those days). I played that VCR tape so many times that I wore it out and actually went and stole another copy of it from a local video store (first and last thing I ever stole in my life).

Eventually my friends and family took notice to my withdrawal from society. The exact cause of my chosen path of isolation was a mystery to them, because I refused to speak about it. Looking back now, I realize that I was a real jerk about the way I treated everyone. Have you ever noticed how much we tend to treat the people who are closest to us the worst when we are suffering inside? It's as if the ones we love become our personal punching bags. I really put my family and friends through the ringer. Thanks to me, my parents learned the meaning of the old saying like speaking to a brick wall. Shutting out the world was my only priority. My absolute refusal to surrender even the slightest hint about what I was going through made the situation ten times worse, because without knowing the cause, they could not begin to help with a solution.

Even the very best of friends have limitations on the amount of grief they will tolerate from their friends. Eventually I pushed mine over the edge to the point where they said the hell with me, (because I simply wasn't worth it). Parents on the other hand, often put up with grief from a child in agony to the point where the stress almost kills them. I gave so much aggravation to my parents that it's no wonder that I did not give them each a stroke or a heart attack. As my stress level grew, so did the intensity of the tongue-lashings I dished out to them. I'm ashamed to admit that on more than one occasion I've brought my parents to tears. Please understand this was more than just your typical teenager having a characteristic bad day or two.

My parents were obviously well aware that I had an eye problem. What they were not aware of was that it had eventually become such a pain in the ass to wear my one remaining contact lenses that I simply chose one day to stop wearing it. Doing so was the equivalent of becoming completely disconnected from whatever part of the world I still had any sort of association with. This was the final brick in my wall of isolation. My eyes became so sensitive to light that I simply stopped going outside during the daylight hours. That was fine by me, because I needed to sleep during the day, since it took me forever at night to finally clear my mind enough to fall asleep anyway. So I adopted a new pattern of sleeping until two or three in the afternoon and not going to bed until around 3am. The crazy thing was, the more that I slept, the more tired I felt when I woke up. From what I understand, I am not alone in experiencing this oddity. I've heard it referred to in theory as sleep inertia. It's my understanding that scientists have yet to determine why oversleeping makes us feel more tired. All I can say is that I can vouch that it is real.

Sometimes after one of those really deep sleeps I would be so groggy upon awakening, that for that split second or two that elapsed before completely opening my eyes, I had actually forgotten that I lost my vision, my desire to do anything, and that my life had turned into a rotten hell. Those tiny microseconds became the only part of my life where I felt that so-glad-to-be-alive euphoria that once dominated my existence. These were nothing more than mere occasional sparks. They were subtle reminders of the raging inferno that was once, (but no longer), my incredibly potent desire to live life to the fullest. But those sparks would be immediately extinguished the moment I caught a glimpse of the distorted view that was now my living hell.

As I previously described, everything around me appeared as one big disgusting blurry blob, with some parts that were constantly moving, even when everything in my field of vision remained completely stationary. I saw a kaleidoscope of objects and colors that was so confusing for my brain to attempt to process, that it took less than five minutes to trigger the onset of a nasty migraine. Viewing any source of light, (whether it was a light bulb, a street light, or the digital display on a television), was like watching a battle scene from the movie Star Wars, (complete with Light sabers, Blasters, and Laser Cannons). Within the streaks of light, traveled what is commonly referred to as floaters. Oddly, I recognized these objects from way back in my junior high school biology class when we conducted our lab work on human blood using microscopes. There was no doubt in my mind that the floaters I could view in my vision were actually clusters of magnified cells. I was sure of this. The disease had caused my astigmatism to become so severe, that my near-sightedness had reached the point where the only objects I could focus upon sharply were my actual cells as they floated across the tear layers on top of my eyes. How pathetic was that?

I'll tell you how pathetic it was; it was so pathetic that it made me, (the not very religious person), actually pray to God to ask him to have mercy on my soul and just get it over with by taking all of my remaining vision. Complete and absolute darkness would have been a much-needed improvement over the little distorted vision that I had left. I prayed for complete blindness, yet God did not deliver, so I took matters into my own hands by searching the house for one of those sleeping masks that my mom had once used to block out light while she slept. My intentions were to wear the mask until the day arrived when I finally went blind all of the way. But as luck would have it, when I found the mask and put it on over my eyes, I discovered that there were now tiny pinholes in the fabric that must have developed with wear and tear. This made me burst out in tears worse than I had ever done before, (even as a baby). I couldn't handle it anymore. It was clear to me that I had the ability to turn even the simplest endeavors into epic failures. My once incredibly promising life had transformed into ruins less than a few months after my eighteenth birthday. I flunked out of college, (ruining my scholarship), got fired from my job, and alienated myself from my friends and family. I smoked, drank, and broke the law. It was no wonder why my girlfriend dumped me for another guy. And, on top of it all, I lost nearly all of my eyesight with not a strand of hope for getting any of it back.

At that point, there was nothing left in my life to be proud of. That amazing dynamic person full of energy, morals and charisma, (who not too long before this emerged from the top of that sandy bluff full of hope and visions), was all but dead. In his place was this self-pitying loser, who was full of excuses and drowning in his own sorrow. This new reality of mine was too much to accept. I was about to make what would have been the absolute last rational conclusion I would ever make in my poor excuse for a life, by accepting that my very existence here on earth was itself a failure of epic proportions.

It was at that precise moment in my short tragic life, (this was indeed arguably my true darkest hour, as I sat there crunched up in a ball in one of the corners of my room in my version of perfect isolation, and on the verge of complete emotional meltdown), that I had a vision that more than likely saved my sanity, and arguably my life. It wasn't the type of vision that comes to mind, like an epiphany. It was an actual, real vision, (like the kind that you see with your eyes!!!). As unlikely as it seems, when I raised my face from my clenches (after crying my eyes out), I was startled by my ability to concentrate clearly upon the number **444,** perfectly in focus in front of me. I immediately recognized this as the time of day being displayed on my digital alarm clock. What made that crystal clear vision most amazing was that the alarm clock was on a nightstand on the complete opposite side of the bedroom!

That is when I discovered how I never removed the sleeping mask from my face. Oddly enough, when I did remove it, the crisp vision immediately disappeared and was replaced by my distorted vision once again. But when I put the mask back over my eyes, I was able to regain the perfect vision by squinting through one of the pinholes in the fabric. 444. I remember thinking to myself what an absolutely beautiful number that is! Why the hell I was able to see it perfectly while squinting through a pinhole was beyond my comprehension at that time. The exact reason didn't matter to me anyway. And surprisingly, neither did any of those mounting problems that were about to get the best of me.

You see, as extraordinary as this may sound, when that magical number 444 came into focus, I could feel my soul being overcome by an incredibly comforting sensation. It was as if I was surrounded my magnificent angels who proceeded to whisper to me that no matter how bad my situation was, or how much worse it still might get, I truly had nothing to fear because in the end everything was going to be alright! The number 444 threw me a much-needed life preserver. It provided me with that valuable strand of hope that I so desperately needed, at a time when I was convinced that hope for me no longer existed. For that I shall forever remain grateful! As you will soon discover, I still had a rocky road ahead, (full of both amazing advances and dreadful setbacks). But, just like during that horrible ordeal following my car accident, it's so much easier to survive the turbulent times when you have something to believe in. For me, hope arrived as an unexpected image of that alarm clock in perfect focus at the time when my outlook seemed to be dark and bleak. The image of 444 glowing across the room became my guiding light. Despite everything I thought I knew about the progression of my vision loss, my unexpected ability to focus perfectly upon the 444 on the alarm clock display by squinting through that pinhole in the mask, was indeed an indication of hope.

Once I cleared the tears from my eyes and allowed my brain enough time to process what I was experiencing, I knew everything was going to be all right. This was because it occurred to me that what felt like an absolute miracle was actually a message from an angel begging me not to give up.

Despite everything all those doctors and their fancy instruments told us about how I would most likely never obtain any useful vision out of my eyes again, the fact of the matter was that the stupid pinhole in that raggedy old mask was able to reveal how my eyes actually never lost the ability to see clearly. It didn't matter that I hadn't a clue why this was. That was something I was going to leave up to the medical field to explain. All I knew was that once again I was reminded how often the simplest solutions to our most complex problems sometimes exist right under our noses. And when we find them... well that's a beautiful thing.

Chapter 9

Someone once asked me to describe the emotional experience of losing my eyesight. At first, I was lost for words. Then it occurred to me; it feels a thousand times worse than losing someone you love under the most unfair of circumstances. Seriously… if you ever had your heart broken because the love of your life suddenly ended your relationship and left you in a harsh and unexpected way or if someone very close to you died suddenly without warning then you are surely aware of this massive pain that I speak of. It's pure, raw, excessive pain (and it hurts even more when it's unjust and unexpected).

I had every intention to describe these awful emotions in the previous chapter. To be honest with you (just like losing that love of your life) the process of putting that chain of events into words in order to write the last chapter stirred up so many horrible emotions (you know, that giant lump in your throat that refuses to go away) that it set me off into a four-month depression. I kid you not. I contest that it just took months for me to pull myself out of that dark place and muster up enough courage to come back here and carry on. Hiding behind the excuse of having writers block, I put this entire project on the back burner to avoid reliving the gut-wrenching wounds all over again. Yet here I sit in the waiting room of an airport hangar typing away on my laptop while my sixteen-year-old son is up in the air for his weekly flying lesson. That giant lump in my throat is still here and my eyes often still become watery as I attempt to hold back the tears. Yet despite the complex emotions, carry on I must.

There is an old saying of unknown origin that goes something like

"It's better to have loved and lost than never to have loved at all."

Well, if losing one's eyesight is a zillion times worse than losing a love then I can say from firsthand experience that one should call into question whether it is indeed better to have lost one's eyesight than to have never been able to see at all. Vision is indeed remarkable but to have it and then to lose it is an unbearable, incomprehensibly painful experience of pure torture and turmoil. Using the phrase complex emotions is nothing short of an understatement for an experience that simply doesn't have words available to do its proper description any sort of justice.

Speaking of complex, losing my mojo surely ranked on the top of my list. Anyone who has ever found themselves hopelessly buried up to their neck in a mountain-sized pile of debt with no way to dig their way out will tell you that the experience leaves a person wanting nothing more than to escape reality. The credit card companies lure us in with their happy-go-lucky advertisements when in reality they are ruthless greedy sons of bitches. They encourage us to transfer high balances with their 0% for 12 months promotional offers. But all it takes is one payment that is a day late to zing us with their 36% (or higher) default rate.

You can try calling their customer service departments to attempt to appeal to their human side (good luck with that endeavor). The bottom line is that without mortgaging the hell out of your home or coming into a huge financial windfall, credit card debt is a bottomless pit that will swallow you whole without any remorse. For someone who isn't accustomed to failure (or to whom failure is not an option), revolving out-of-control debt is a burden that isn't easy to carry.

With a family depending upon me, any sort of failure of epic proportions seemed completely out of the question. Watching the great life that I had worked so hard to build falling apart before my very eyes surely ranked at the top of the list of what I would define as epic. It didn't take a financial wizard to see how I was on a collision course to lose the house and my ability to provide food, clothing and other essentials. Our household budget depended upon my ability to sustain a steady stream of income. Working on commission might come with the potential for some handsome rewards. But it also comes with a great deal of risk. After many years of success, I never imagined that I would ever find myself struggling so greatly. It didn't take long for the frustration to get the best of me. Once again, my mind drifted into that dark ugly secluded land of loneliness. The only difference was that this time when I tried to escape the real world by sleeping my life away (as I did when I lost my vision), instead of finding that much needed peaceful tranquility in my dreams, I instead started to experience some really strange nightmares.

The nightmares were frightening enough to wake me up in a cold sweat in the middle of the night. Each one of those nightmares had the same theme. In dreamland I was the keeper of a horrible secret. When those nightmares first began to occur I would awaken before the plot would develop enough to discover what that terrible secret was. But as the dreams replayed the plot and storyline thickened. Once it did, I regretted my curiosity. You see, the best that I could tell, that horrible secret in my dreams appeared to be the knowledge of the location of a buried dead body!

It's my understanding that some people are fortunate enough to not ever have to experience graphic nightmares. If you are one of those people... well you have no idea how lucky you are. Otherwise, you are surely familiar with how realistic graphic nightmares can be. I know for me all of my senses and emotions are intensified during my heart-pounding nightmares. I feel and experience everything with such intense awareness that sometimes I often confuse my dreamland memories with those of the real world.

I've come to accept the torturous experience of explicitly remembering nightmares as a trade-off for my ability to do the same with some very good dreams too. Sometimes I find amazing awards in the happy dreams (such as pleasant revelations or incredibly creative ideas). There is no doubt in my mind that my ability to recall and describe the particulars of most of my dreams is indeed a gift of some sorts. Whether it's a good or bad gift is a topic open for debate. It's easy to view it as some sort of incredible natural talent. But when one of those nightmares would wake me in the middle of the night in a full-blown anxiety attack (and so choked-up that I could not stop the tears from flowing) I view that gift as nothing more than a severely incapacitating mental handicap.

Now before your mind starts spinning, please erase any suspicion that I am some sort of psychopath mass murderer. Here on Long Island we already have had our fair share of serial killers so the island does not need another (even as I write this chapter it appears that yet another one has emerged as the local police are uncovering the bodies of dead prostitutes from the shadows of our ocean dunes). So set the record straight by understanding that many times the objects we dream about are often symbolic and not to be taken literally.

With that being said, that which appeared to represent a secret buried body in my dreams really scared the hell out of me. The dreamland plot was sketchy in how it purposely made it unclear whether or not I was responsible for the victim's demise. I do know that in my dreams I walked around with loads of guilt and shame (so I must have been involved in at least the act of concealing the body from the world). If I had to take an educated crack at deciphering what those nightmares (and the concept of the buried body) may have stood for, I would say that the dead body most likely symbolized my financial trouble and the way I concealed it from everyone around me. One could easily argue that I irresponsibly murdered my credit when I let my pride stand in the way of being frugal (I guess you could even call it financial suicide!). And if that dead body indeed symbolized my credit then the heartless vultures in

152

my dreams undoubtedly represented the ruthless banks who issued my credit cards. All I know is that walking around with the guilt of falling in massive debt is painstakingly familiar to the way I felt in those nightmares about that hidden corpse.

Today it's easy to draw these conclusions about the likely interpretation of those dreams. Back in the day when they were occurring was a different story. Knowing that something was obviously wrong with my mind, I could not rule out the remote possibility that the dreams were actually some sort of prediction of what the future could bring had I remained on the destructive course on which I was heading. Worse yet, (even though I could not bring myself to admit its possibility) there was also the possibility that the nightmares were actually suppressed memories (no matter how out-of-character for me it would have been to have been involved with such extreme foul play). Either way, both of those alternative notions frightened the hell out of me.

What made matters even worse was the sense of familiarity I felt about the general storyline. When the dreams first started, I simply assumed that the familiarity was strictly due to my memories of how the body of one of my fellow classmates back in high school turned up in some woods in our neighborhood a few years after she had gone missing. To the best of my knowledge, that mystery was never solved. Rumor has it that some of that classmate's friends panicked when she overdosed while doing illegal drugs with them so it was rumored that they rolled her body up in an old carpet and dumped her in that patch of woods in our neighborhood (rather than risking being held responsible for her death).

I thought I might have been possibly dreaming about the guilt that was being felt by her friends (who to this day have to walk around with that dark secret imbedded in their memory banks if that rumor is true). As children, my friends and I often played in those woods. We were all well aware of the rolled-up carpet. We just weren't smart enough to put two and two together to figure out that the carpet actually contained a dead body. Death and decay emit the most horrendous smell (worse than you can ever imagine). I learned this from my wilderness escapades. In addition to all of the time I spent camping and hiking with the scouts, I also spent many summers in the Catskill Mountains where my maternal grandfather built a country home for the family. When we were children, my uncle (who is very close to my age) and I had an entire mountain range as a playground.

If you spend a decent amount of time in the wilderness you are bound to eventually come across a decaying animal carcass or two. There is no mistaking the unique foul odor of decomposing flesh and organs (and the colony of maggots feasting upon it) or the roaring symphony emitted by the beating wings of the hundreds of flies hovering in the air above. Just the thought of it turns my stomach. If the weather is warm and the remains are fresh, that horrendous stench and the telltale sound is usually detected long before the source is within view. That was the case when I was with my friends playing in the woods near that rolled-up carpet. We were smart enough to detect that there was something dead nearby. But we just assumed the smell was from another dead raccoon, squirrel or opossum. It's not like the bodies of dead teenagers were commonly found anywhere near our town so none of us ever gave that rolled up carpet much thought. To us it appeared to be nothing more than just another one of those soggy, moldy, rolled-up carpets we've seen situated amongst other illegally dumped junk within the labyrinth of trails in those woods (and many other patches of woods that served as places we visited to retreat from the hustle and bustle of suburbia, USA).

If the overdose story is true (as most of the neighborhood accepted it to be), then the teenagers who covered up that girl's death surely lived their lives fearing that dreadful knock on the door from the police. The relentless fear of being caught when you know that you are guilty is so consuming that it can eat away your soul. This is the exact feeling I was experiencing in my dreams night after night. The crazy thing was (as I described earlier), until the injury to my frontal lobe healed, I was left with the inability to feel guilt or shame in the real world. Yet, in dreamland (and the few moments that ensued after awaking from nightmares) I was overcome with it. This confused me a bit because when I made that realization, I had to wonder if I actually felt any guilt at all about being in debt and heading toward a head-on collision with bankruptcy. That made me consider the possibility that my psyche was letting out emotions in dreamland simply because I was unable to reap the benefits of releasing them in the real world. I know this is real deep psycho-analytical stuff (and I'm far from being any sort of qualified expert in that field) so please excuse me if I'm making your head spin a bit.

As the storyline of my nightmares progressed, I eventually discovered that I was not dreaming about the mysteriously dumped body of my classmate. You see, in my nightmares, the body was concealed under concrete steps in front of a home somewhere in Brooklyn. I guess from a symbolic standpoint, that location was most fitting. Steps allow us to safely and methodically ascend to higher places. We all know that concrete is symbolic of a strong foundation. So how fitting is it to theorize that buried within the strong foundation that I utilized to climb to where I am today in life are the skeletons of my past struggles with debt. Once again, I don't know if any of this makes any sense. All I know is that as time went on, the anxiety caused by those nightmares only continued to intensify until it prevented me from living my life normally. When the nightmares were taking place, I wasn't clear-headed enough to realize the symbolism. I was simply a guy who was having some very sick dreams.

Sometimes I would find myself in situations where my heart would be racing and my blood pressure would be boiling because characters in the dreams would come uncomfortably close to discovering my involvement in the disappearance of the imaginary dead body. Other times I would dream about being in confrontations with fictitious dreamland characters who were also involved in the sinister plot. It may have been an imaginary buried corpse but at the time of those nightmares it sure felt possible that it was real. As a matter of fact, it felt so real that my heart would race whenever I would see a police officer or a patrol car in the real world. I was a perfectly innocent man who has never intentionally harmed another human being during my entire life yet there I was experiencing anxiety like an escaped convict on the run. It was as if my conscious was afraid of being caught for the secret crime that the dreamland me committed in those nightmares. How sick is that?

Eventually I started to discover a direct correlation between my financial troubles and the frequency (and intensity) of my nightmares. For instance, on days when I was hounded more than usual with harassing phone calls from heartless bill collectors, the evening nightmares were proportionately more intense. But without seeing the symbolism, I simply assumed that my nightmares were more intense on more stressful days. And since sleepless nights created more stressful days, I found myself caught within a hopeless loop without any escape. For someone who reached the point where I was literally hanging on to my sanity by a thread, the unwelcome addition of those nightmares to the mix was enough to convince me that I was never going to see another happy, stress-free day in my life. It's a shame how when put to the test, most of us fail to keep tabs on what is truly important in life. On the top of the list should always remain the health and safety of the people we love. Next should come oneself. If the welfare of our loved ones and oneself are safe and sound, nothing else truly should matter, should it?

Well, that is easier said than done. The truth is that we live in a world where we can easily lose sight of the things that are really important to us. To make matters worse, when our minds and hearts are consumed with disgust as we watch things not going the way that we hoped, we tend to unfortunately misdirect our anger toward the people who are closest to us. If our emotions are too intense, we can quickly alienate ourselves from our loved ones (and the rest of the world). Nobody wants to be someone else's punching bag or pin cushion. When we crap on someone we love for no logical reason, nine times out of ten we do it because of misdirected emotions. Then, when we run out of loved-ones to abuse (because we pushed them all away) the only person left to beat up are ourselves. This is clearly a recipe for self-destruction.

I would be lying to you if I told you that I've mastered a way to stop misdirecting my anger. Truth be told, I'm horrible at it. The only thing that I have to offer in this regard is a boatload of examples of what not to do. For instance, you should know that no matter how bad a stressful situation becomes, there will never become a point where it is considered so bad that lashing out to your loved-ones is an acceptable way to blow off some steam. No amount of stress will ever justify misdirecting anger. Likewise, withdrawal is not an acceptable way to counteract your urges to place unwarranted blame on your spouse or children as a means of relieving a burden that you should be carrying on your shoulders alone. Giving them the silent treatment because you are afraid of the damaging words that might come out of your mouth involuntarily is almost as bad as actually saying the words. With that in mind, I'm sure that the best solution lies in that middle ground that occupies the space in between. What I'm not sure of is how to pinpoint the absolute best way to harness our actions and keep them pegged down the center path between not-too-much and not-too-little.

For what it's worth, the experience of going through the worst of times allows us to truly learn who we are and what we are capable of. Life is full of hundreds of ways to measure people based upon our performances when we are most successful. I have a wall full of plaques and trophies that are a reflection of all of the moments in my career when I attained greatness. Superficially, those awards can surely be perceived to define me and my ability. But our perception and methods of recognizing accomplishments is in many ways upside down. The true rewards should be given for the periods of time when we had to dig really deep to find the strength to lift ourselves off of the ground and push ourselves from rock bottom to all the way back to the top of our game.

There are many people who are lucky enough to find themselves right smack in the middle of successful situations. Sometimes people are born into a world where everything they need for success is handed to them effortlessly. Other times people simply find themselves in the right place at the right time (also effortlessly). What each of those people are lacking is a matter of substance behind their success stories. For a runt of the litter like me, you would think that it would be extremely frustrating to be in the same room as the folks who were basically handed their success while I had to grind it out every step of the way. I have to tell you that it's not like that at all. When you rely on your own hard work, intelligence, and dedication (and are able to move mountains as a result), the respect that your success commands know no boundaries. So when I walk into a room full of other highly successful individuals I can hold my head up high with confidence because I know that my accomplishments came as a result of my battles through the darkest of times.

There are many people who use the expression of being through hell and back. I've been there, done that and actually have the battles wounds (both physical and emotional) to prove it. In contrast, I've been fortunate enough to have been to some of the most beautiful places on earth. Having such a broad spectrum of experiences to compare others to, I can easily say (without hesitation) that the darkest, most sinister places I have ever visited were within my very own mind. The world indeed has its fair share of dark cruel places. However, no matter how horrible the real world is at times, most individuals always have the tranquil spaces within their own minds to escape to (sleeping being on top of the list). But as I quickly learned, when the troubles of the real world are equally matched (or worse yet, overshadowed) by stress from our psyche and dreamland, there truly is no place left for us to hide (I now know why some troubled people literally drink themselves to death with alcohol).

It's not just the major stuff that bogs us down and prevents us from carrying on normal, healthy lives. When we go through these sorts of traumatic events it becomes rather easy for us to get hung up on the small defeats and all of the pesky nuisances that also come as part of the package. This usually makes it even more difficult for us to cope with the situation. Then, almost like clockwork, someone always comes along to tell us how all bad things happen for a reason (and how that reason is not always obvious at the time we are experiencing a bad event). I've always known about this concept yet I probably never gave it as much thought as it deserves (until now). Naturally, it's easy to see (after the fact) how one of the reasons for experiencing my life falling apart as a result of going blind was to prepare me for when my life fell apart after my car accident. I cannot deny the similarities. Then again, there is an entire school of thought out there that firmly believes in the concept that Shit Happens.

The thing about being an optimist is that we tend to avoid getting caught up in answering the questions that pertain to why bad things happen. But one of the problems we face is that there is no such thing as a 100% pure optimist. That means that even the most extreme optimist has a small pessimist hidden inside. Like it or not, that little pessimist has a voice. Obviously, he offers a conflicting opinion to what the optimist has to say. What makes us such positive-minded people is how we most often carry on our lives without giving that little pessimist much credit. Under ordinary circumstances, I simply block him out. That's really easy to do when the pessimist's voice is weak and his opinion lacks any noteworthy credibility.

However, when faced with trouble (especially really big trouble), the optimist inside our heads is often beaten up. When this happens, we are tested by the fact that this gives the pessimist inside us the opportunity to speak his mind. It's a power struggle (and credibility equals power). Ever hear someone say that they have some soul searching to do? Well, nine times out of ten, this means that the person needs time to figure out which of the two voices to listen to (or how much credit to give each of them). Some individuals tend to be in a constant state of confusion and indecisiveness. But sometimes the events in our lives unfold in such a way that even the most sure-minded personalities can lose their bearings.

If you are familiar with famous literature then you are surely aware of the fact that this battle of morals within a person's mind is often the basis for many plots because of how intense the struggle can become. Even the most seasoned soldiers will admit how it takes a much stronger warrior to conquer and survive the battles within our mind than it does even the most trying physical challenges. Like it or not, the traumatic experiences of losing my eyesight as well as losing my mojo put me right smack in the center of this conflict. And living in this "what-have-you-done-lately?" world of ours, it wasn't easy to deal with the inner conflict at the same time as trying to deal with the outside pressures. It's a tight race between which is worse too; the struggles within our own conscience or the struggles with the outside world. I'm not too sure which one is worse.

Chapter 10

A pinhole occlude is a dark disk with at least one if not several small holes through it. It's a device that is used by ophthalmologists to test visual acuity. It works very similar to the way that a pinhole camera focuses a tiny lighted image on to a larger piece of film. It works by taking away all the other reflective light around the object that is being focused upon so that the retina in the back of the eye is able to see what is within the pinhole more clearly. It's the absence of all the surrounding light that allows the object being viewed through one of the holes in the pinhole occlude to come into focus.

I knew none of this until I described my miraculous experience of obtaining vision through the pinholes in the sleeping mask. My ability to see clear images again was duplicated in a doctor's office by squinting through one of the pinholes in a pinhole occlude. I was being told that the device can be used to measure and determine what would and could potentially be an eye's absolute best vision obtainable using corrective lenses. For me, that translated into 20/15 vision in each eye (which basically means that at 20 feet away I could see the best vision that a person was expected to see on the eye chart by standing only 15 feet away). In other words, each of my eyes possessed the potential to obtain 'better than normal' vision.

Now here was the dilemma... the eye doctors on Long Island were able to determine that my eyes could obtain that excellent vision but what they couldn't determine was how to go about making that happen. You see, at this point the astigmatism in my eyes were so bad that scar tissue formed across and around my corneas from the tissue rapidly stretching so quickly over what amounted to be a relatively short period of time. Today we have laser surgery that can be utilized to correct minor astigmatism. Back in the late 1980s laser eye surgery sounded like something out of a science fiction novel. The astigmatism in my eyes was so bad that even with modern laser surgery capabilities there was no way that a laser would be able to also remove the scar tissue and flatten out the cones of my corneas enough for me to obtain any sort of useful vision.

Talk about a rollercoaster of emotions. The freak 444 pinhole experience gave me so much hope but hearing the discouraging words of one doctor after another (it literally felt like I had visited every eye specialist on the entire island) was nothing short of demoralizing and deflating. I would dig myself a few inches out of depression only to be swallowed up and dragged down many feet after every doctor's visit. But as life would have it (being so full of twists and unexpected turns) my godsend saving grace would come from no other than my Brooklyn roots. Once word got out among the people I knew about my condition, rumors of old-timers from the Brooklyn neighborhood with homemade PINHOLE glasses began to surface!

"The old Italian eye disease." that's what I first heard it referred to from several different (and unrelated) sources. I steadily began to learn that I was not alone with my struggles with this eye disorder. It became apparent to me that had I been born in the 1920s or 30s my situation would have been hopeless. More common stories were surfacing of great uncles, cousins, etc. from those eras who lost their vision as teenagers (in the same manner as I did) only to spend the rest of their lives struggling with soda-bottle thick eyeglasses, magnifying glasses and for those who were lucky enough to discover the secret; pinhole spectacles. Lucky for me, I was born in the 1960s and modern medicine for my generation in the 1980s had a fix for my condition. It was a fix that not one of those doctors on Long Island had any knowledge of. No, it took a trip to an elderly Italian ophthalmologist (whose office ironically was in Brooklyn) for me to receive an immediate diagnosis. The man spoke broken English and often used non-medical terminology (such as "the Italian eye disease") but when push came to shove he pointed to the word Keratoconus in a shiny new Ophthalmology medical dictionary that was so new to his bookshelf that it still had the price sticker on the cover. And just like that the gears were put in motion as I was set on the road to a cure.

When asked what the cure was, the jolly old Italian guru chuckled and said the words:

"You go see my friend Jorge in Manhattan and he get you new eyes."

Those words were the last words I expected to hear (mostly because everyone knew that eye transplants were not a real thing) but hidden within that phrase there was indeed mostly truths. His friend Jorge in Manhattan was the world-renowned Dr. Jorge Buxton of the New York Eye and Ear Infirmary. Dr. Buxton's specialty was perfecting the art of cornea transplants. The new eyes that were spoken of were the new set of corneas that would eventually allow me to wear those very special contact lenses which in turn would eventually allow me to once again achieve 20-20 and better vision out of each eye. The road ahead was not without some major twists and turns but it was at least pointed in the right direction and I was placed on it right as I thought there was no hope. All this came about because of the freak 444 pinhole experience.

It's quite bizarre how one moment we can be in a full-blown panic as we fall out of control down into a dark bottomless pit and moments later, we can have a hand with a solid grip on the surface with our feet firmly planted into footholds. The moment we discover that escape ladder (the one that was always there, and we just didn't see it) the panic is instantly turned into serenity. It's one big giant HAH-HAH moment where we whisper to ourselves the words:

"Everything is going to be alright."

From that moment onward, it didn't matter much what the challenges were that I faced with regaining my vision. What mattered to me was that I WAS regaining my vision and once I set on that course nothing else really mattered. I can write chapters upon chapters about the struggles that ensued along the way but why bother? I'm sure many people would find it heartbreaking to hear how my first cornea transplant... the very first hope at regaining my vision was a complete failure due mainly to my own actions. I am sure many people would find it entertaining to hear the story about the time that I accidentally placed several large drops of instant Super Glue into one of my eyes (thinking that it was a bottle of prescription eye drops). I kid you not that this truly occurred.

More important to mention first is that no matter how good things are going there are always going to be times when we are still bullied by life just as there are always going to be times when we are still blind in one way or another. It's ever important to drill home these facts by opening eyes and minds to realize that our paths will always come upon obstacles. Obstacles are inevitable. Some of us travel paths that are smoother going than others at times but when you look at the overall journeys that each of us take you will often see that it all balances out in the end. Long periods of smooth sailing seas are often replaced with long periods of stormy weather. And no matter how big or small we need to realize that every obstacle has a specific method that we need to choose to deal with it. Some obstacles we can push right through the way a ship cuts through an angry sea or the way a bulldozer plows over a mound of dirt. Other obstacles are more difficult and can't simply be manhandled. Some require a great deal of time and energy to find an alternate route around them while others simply need to be dealt with because they will never go away. Obstacles will pop up just as clear skies can quickly give way to a fog that rolls in and destroys our visibility of the horizon. Learning to deal with them creates life lessons that we carry with us for as long as we walk this Earth.

We all have our struggles and our struggles are real. Life finds a way to bully each of us.

Sometimes we are fortunate enough to have a guru to help guide us through or around the obstacles we face. Other times we accidentally stumble upon those freak 444 pinhole experiences that lead us on a path that we had no idea we would ever take. And sometimes, often, we are faced with obstacles that for an extended period leave us feeling hopeless. Hopelessness is no joke. It's that black hole that sucks you in and gives you no indication that there even exists a single foothold to grab on to. If you are fortunate enough to have not experienced this state of mind yet in your life than you will have to trust those who have. If you cannot comprehend how anyone can feel so hopeless that they decide that the best solution to their sorrow is to end it by ending their own life, then you are indeed among the truly fortunate.

Hopelessness is the leading cause of suicidal thoughts. For many individuals, that sensation of falling helplessly down that black hole is too much for them to handle. It's so scary that it's painful. The pain is so intense that it turns to numbness. The numbness is so widespread that it distorts the mind and plays games with reason and common sense until suicide appears to be the only reasonable solution to end the anguish and stop the viscous cycle. Pulling someone out of the depths of one of those black holes is never the same experience because no two black holes are the same such as no two obstacles are the same experience. Sometimes all it takes a helping hand, some kind words of encouragement or a simple prescription to lift someone out of the abyss. Other times it can consume a lifetime of effort only to still fail in the end.

I have this theory that we are all mentally ill in some way, shape or form. Not one of us is 100% mentally healthy. With that in mind it's easy to understand that each of us possess a different capacity for coping with the obstacles that we face. At different times in our lives we might be stronger or weaker than at other times. This adds yet another layer of uncertainty to how well we can or cannot deal with the obstacles that block our paths. The other variable that nobody ever considers is the fact that when you are riding an emotional rollercoaster with very steep peaks and valleys, the lows feel much lower than what they may really be because we experience them in a short period of time after the highs so they are in sharp contrast to each other.

The moment I learned that my body rejected my first cornea transplant I experienced one of those sharply contrasting lows. Like any transplant surgery there is always the risk of rejection. In my case (and unknown to my doctors) my immune system was simply too strong.

Even while using anti-rejection steroid medication my immune system was sharp enough to recognize that there were foreign cells attached to my eye. My body marched in white blood cells like a D-Day invasion on the shores of France by the allied forces. And this did not occur immediately after the surgery. No, it had to happen after I had to experience months of agony having dozens of sutures removed by tweezers at my weekly follow-up visits. I endured that torture because it was one leg on the road to recovery but the thought that it was all wasted... the thought that it all had to be repeated a second time contributed to the free-fall back down into that black hole of depression. Imagine how I must have felt regaining my vision only to lose it again in such a sudden and unexpected way after months of progressive recovery.

Freefalling into darkness. Yes, that is what it feels like. Interview anyone who is suffering from uncontrollable hopelessness and they will describe it in this very same manner. For most individuals it's the fear that the black hole is indeed a bottomless abyss. However, there is a unique group of twisted, dark-minded individuals who found the energy, courage and know-how to embrace the darkness. For them the darkness defines who they are. In their world they've free-fallen so long that they came to the revelation that there is indeed a bottom to the black hole just as there truly is a bottom to every lake that is nicknamed a bottomless lake. What's even more remarkable is that you'd expect them to describe the landing as a messy crash when in fact they will tell you that the abyss has a soft mushy bottom that absorbs the high-speed impact of the free-fall. Once these individuals regain their footing at the bottom of the self-pity tavern this is where many of them choose to live out their lives. For some unknown reason, once they arrive, they don't want to leave.

Me personally, I never made it to the bottom. I always assumed the term 'rock bottom' was the valid description of the fate that I would meet if I were to continue to fall into the darkness at such a high speed. The fear of impact was a good percentage of the nightmare. Not being able to see what existed below me was another good part of it. There was never any indication that the ability to land at the bottom and still exist was even an option. To me it felt as though I was falling to my death. I cannot grasp my head around what level of courage it must take to decide to just go with the fall instead of fighting it. This is the exact reason why suicide is defined as a cowardly act. Those who take their lives do so because they cannot tolerate the fear of impact any longer. This is also the reason why those whose chose to live out their lives dwelling at the bottom of the black hole are anything but suicidal.

Yes, it's true. They might dress in black; they might be labeled 'emotional' or 'gothic' but just because they find greatness in things that the general population might consider dark or mysterious doesn't mean they are suicidal. Of course, there are always exceptions to the rule but for the most part if you have a loved one who you are concerned about because they suffer from social anxiety and they don't fancy bright colors or normal humor but rather they find themselves drawn toward isolation and all things dark and lonely, you probably don't need to be concerned about that person taking their own life. They aren't searching for that sort of escape because their free-fall already ended with a landing at the bottom of their own abyss. They don't suffer from hopelessness in the same manner as someone who is truly suicidal amid an unbearable free-fall would be.

Sometimes I wonder how my life would have turned-out if I didn't suffer from this dreaded eye disease. Of course, I would have had other struggles to deal with throughout my years but none of what I've experienced has come anywhere close to the ordeal I was handed when I inherited the keratoconus gene defect. I often wonder if I would have been more, or less successful in my career, in my relationships and in life in general. The more I think about it the more I realize that even though it was an experience that I never would want to have to go through again, the struggles riding that emotional rollercoaster have, for the most part, defined my very existence and molded me into who I am today. I am contempt and if given a choice I wouldn't change a single part of my past. I've come to accept that the scars of my past are reminders of what I can accomplish when put to the test. They are also reminders that I am not perfect and that I can and will make mistakes (and I make them often).

The Super Glue story is a perfect example of how one can have good intentions and still make a horrible (and potentially life-changing) mistake. It occurred in a dimly lit Mexican restaurant immediately after one of my follow-up visits with Dr. Buxton. Like every other visit, my mother was my escort because I was still legally blind. Every week for two years my mom would escort me on the Long Island Railroad to Penn station and then a taxi-ride downtown to the New York Eye and Ear Infirmary on 14th street and 2nd avenue. We did this in the scorching heat of summer as well as during blustery snowstorms in the winter and torrential downpours in the Spring. My eye appointments were a necessity and having my mom with me was a godsend because sometimes that doctor's instructions with my prescriptions and eye care were long and intense. Having a second set of ears often made a big difference.

That week I had accidentally scratched my right cornea by rubbing my eye after wind had blown some sand into it. The doctor had prescribed an antibiotic eye drop to prevent infection while the abrasion healed. Prescribing antibiotics for someone with a cornea transplant is like walking a tightrope because an antibiotic's purpose is to awaken the body's immune system to fight off infection. In my case my immune system is the enemy of my transplanted corneas. Too much antibiotics could awaken the immune system too much causing it to discover the transplanted tissue.

Well we ordered our food in the restaurant and it was time for me to apply the antibiotic drops to my injured eye. Dr. Buxton's office had given the small plastic container to my mother who in turn placed it in her purse. But unknown to either of us my mom reached into her purse and pulled out a bottle of fingernail glue that is used to attach artificial acrylic fingernails. The formula for fingernail glue is the same as your typical quick-drying Super Glue. The bottle that the glue is sold in is ironically the same size and shape as the bottle that contained the antibiotic solution. The only difference was the label and the plastic lid. This was the first time I was applying these new eye drops so I had no expectations of what the bottle or lid should've felt like just as my mom had no expectations of what the bottle or the lid should have looked like. Add that to the fact that I was legally blind and that we were sitting in a dimly lit restaurant and you have the recipe for pure disaster.

I tilted my head back and applied two large drops to the top of my cornea.

IMMEDIATELY I knew something was wrong. I felt my entire eye shrivel and instantly my eye lids and lashes were fused together. My Mom erupted in shear panic as we both realized what had happened. If you are squirming in your seat right now, then be for-warned that this story becomes even more squeamish because anyone who has

173

ever used super glue and has gotten it on their hands knows that there is only one antidote that is used to remove instant super glue and that is no other than 'Acetone nail polish remover'. So as awful as it was experiencing the sensation of applying super glue to my already scratched transplanted cornea the sensation was only paralleled by the doctor having to eventually pour Acetone around and into my eye to first separate my eye lids then to remove the sheets of dried glue that had adhered to the surface of my cornea transplant.

One would think that suffering through such an experience was pure hell. Truth be told, being the optimist I am, I was calm and collected. My first thoughts were that I was going to be permanently blind in that eye. For someone who was already legally blind it wasn't that far of a leap to accept that maybe I was going to only regain the vision in my other eye. That ounce of hope was enough to get me through the entire ordeal. I didn't have a single negative thought toward my mom. I didn't blame her because I was just as guilty and a contributor to the situation. It honestly could have happened to anyone. Remarkably, Dr. Buxton was able to remove all the glue using a bottle of Acetone that my mom picked up at a drug store down the street. And even more remarkably within a few weeks my eye healed well enough that it was undetectable that any trauma ever occurred. Unfortunately, none of that made any difference because a few months later I lost that new cornea to rejection by my immune system.

For me I think the worst part was my feeling of remorse for the person who donated the cornea. I still walk around with the guilt that my first cornea transplant in my right eye was rejected. The donor was a young father in his late 20s who was killed in a car accident. He or his spouse made the generous decision to donate his organs and his corneas and lucky for me, he and I were a good match for the transplant. I know that I cannot control the intensity of my immune system so the rejection may not have been my fault. However, I was a nineteen-year-old kid with a newfound hope. My recent climb out of that black hole of hopelessness left me with a new desire to socialize and reconnect with my friends. Those renewed connections for a teenager translated into drinking beer, staying out late and missing sleep. That unfortunately translated into a recipe for increasing my risk of straining my eyes. Strained eyes = red eyes. Red eyes = more blood flow around the transplanted cornea. More blood flow = increase of a chance that my immune system grew wise of the foreign cells that were sewn into my eye where my original cornea once stood. All said and done I could easily blame myself for wasting that young father's donated cornea. Whether or not my actions truly contributed to the destruction of that cornea will never be known for sure but in my mind, I convinced myself that they did.

The attack came in the middle of a hot summer night. The troops (aka my white blood cells) flooded the transplanted cornea through a blood vessel that travelled upward from the sclera (white of the eye) and into the cornea. Once the connection was made to the cornea my immune system sent in the troops and my once perfectly clear new cornea fogged over from the huge congregation of white blood cells attacking the foreign tissue. Dr. Buxton did all that he could to attempt to reverse the effects of the attack using heavy doses of topical steroids with names like Prednisolone Acetate Ophthalmic Suspension in combination with oral steroids with names like Decadron and Cyclosporine. But despite his best efforts, that new cornea was ruined and so were my dreams of being able to place a rigid gas permeable contact lens on top of it to regain my lost vision. I HAD GONE BLIND FOR A SECOND TIME. I was instantly kicked back into my hole of hopelessness and this time the freefall felt like it was accelerating at a pace that I could not halt.

Chapter 11

If the Earth's gravity is exponentially less the further astronauts sour in altitude away from the Earth, then likewise it's exponentially greater the further we fall into that pit of darkness. If the stronger gravitational pull downward into the abyss isn't enough, then add to that fact that living among the darkness are demons whose only goal is to pull us down deeper and never let us escape. Phobias such as the fear of the dark are a joke compared to the awareness that there are constantly invisible monstrous creepy arms clawing at us. They flourish in the abyss pulling us down deeper and deeper. If you have not experienced what it feels like to have this constant pressure applied to your body, mind and soul then consider yourself extremely fortunate. These creatures are the ultimate bullies and the abyss is their playground. Keeping it all together when a monster is attempting with all his might to tear you apart is no easy feat. Attempting to do it in the dark while free-falling... well that's practically surreal. Talk about a real head and spirit spinner... I was lost never to be found and all I wanted was for my feet or hands to touch some sort of ground. It almost sounds like the lyrics to some mad heavy metal song.

There then comes a moment when I realized that I've become cumbersome to the world and naturally that meant that I became cumbersome to myself. When you are in this situation, you can attempt to transform into a pretender to hide your situation from those around you the best you can. It sometimes works for a short period of time or around strangers who don't know you very well but for anyone who knew the real you it's a hopeless cause because they will see right through your lies and charades. The voices inside your head are so loud that those who know and love you will hear their screams. You see, when you walk the world with a beast strapped to your back embedding its claws into your soul it's not like your people aren't going to notice something is wrong. Pretend all you want… it's a hopeless waste of energy.

I needed to be saved. Never in my life would I ever have imagined that a time would come when I needed saving. Even when I was bullied as a child I never felt as though I needed to be saved. I simply lived with the shame of being bullied. What a wicked game life can be. For an optimist I was down to a few strands of hope to hold on to. I was still alive. That was a good thing, right? I still possessed the ability to process independent thoughts. Independent thoughts in many ways equals freedom. I had been dwelling on that as a positive for a very long time. It's easier to do when you are crushing goals while chasing dreams. In contrast when even having a single aspiration is a far distant dream itself… well that's a messed-up situation with no sign of a doorway or lifeline out.

Call me a hypocrite for being such a self-proclaimed optimist with such dark pessimistic thoughts. It all comes down to limits and what we can tolerate/live with. Call me what you wish for allowing the creatures of the dark penetrate my perspective on life and on the world. If I were one of the seven dwarfs, I clearly thought I was Happy yet one day I woke up in the body of Grumpy and there wasn't a single heroic action in my entire arsenal that could change that revelation. Both critics as well as supporters would share the same common advice for someone in my situation:

"Sleep on it."

Easier said than done though. How does one who can't sleep due to the weight of the world on his shoulders and the fear of impact from the free-falling into the abyss simply sleep on it?

How does one who is experiencing heart-pounding nightmares simply sleep on it?

I remember thinking to myself...

"What a joke!"

Then there is the quicksand factor: The deeper I fell into the abyss the thicker the air became until it reached the point where it felt as thick as quicksand and possessed the same properties. And most of us are fully aware of the rule of quicksand:

The more you move while sinking, the quicker you will sink.

When you've fallen that deep into the darkness there are new rules to follow in addition to the rule of quicksand. For anyone reading this who's experienced the freefall you know that this translates into sleeping all day and still feeling exhausted when you wake up.

It translates into feeling full after not eating for twenty hours straight.

It translates into being lonely while at the same time feeling disturbed the moment another human attempts to communicate one sentence to you.

It translates into all the weight of anyone attempting to assist you falling on you and bringing you down.

And the final translation… the one that hurts everyone around you the most, is that it translates into becoming an angry, irritable, asshole.

I wear my anger on my sleeve. I was an irritable asshole when I first went blind but it was ten times worse when I went blind the second time (when my first cornea transplant rejected). It got so bad that my mom began blaming the steroid eye medications that were being prescribed to me to suppress my immune system to make my body more receptable to receiving transplants.

She got this idea from the well-known fact that athletes and bodybuilders who take metabolic steroids to build their muscles often experience irritability as a side effect. She had a valid argument that even Dr. Buxton entertained for a hot moment. He started to instruct me to pinch the corners of the top of my nose after administering the steroid drops in my eyes. His logic was that the liquid steroids were draining into my sinuses where they could have been quickly absorbed into my blood stream on a direct passage to my brain much like a cocaine user who snorts the nose candy to receive an immediate reaction.

Wearing your anger on your sleeve when you are a loner is one thing. Wearing your anger on your sleeve when you are in a relationship takes on an entirely new meaning. When I went blind the first time it was no wonder that my girlfriend left me for her best friend's boyfriend.

Was it my fault?

Back then I would have answered that question with a bunch of excuses and what if scenarios. Today I simply take full responsibility by stating that it most likely was my fault.

Was it avoidable?

Probably not. An eighteen or nineteen-year-old girl has lots of aspirations. Dealing with the drama of a newly blind boyfriend with a piss-ass attitude surely wasn't one of them. Unfortunately for my children (as you probably figured-out by now), the same fate was in stored for my marriage (although it took another dozen or so years of hell and turmoil for it to completely fall apart).

"We stayed together for the children until they were grown…"

How often have you heard that phrase come from the lips of a divorcee?

Whenever an individual goes through a major implosion there is always going to be reciprocal damages. In our case I was normally the rock. I was the glue that held what was already an unstable relationship together. So, when I hit the point where I couldn't hold myself together there was no energy (or patience) left for me to hold the instability together too. Add to that the clear fact that I was surely acting like a frustrated, short-tempered prick and our relationship didn't stand a chance of surviving. In a perfect world, perhaps my ex-wife would have recognized the turmoil I was going through and she would have come to my rescue. But that never happened, and I will leave it at that without pointing fingers or making excuses. Even the extreme optimist knows that the world has limitations on what others can contribute and that not every real-life drama has a fairytale ending like in the movies.

There are no winners in divorce (other than the attorneys who get rich off the misfortune of others) but there surely are losers and those losers are always inevitably the children. Our three children reacted in their own unique ways (as children will usually do). If I had but one regret with going through the entire divorce/break-up process is that I should have expended more energy preserving my relationships with each of my children. The divorce could not have been easy for them to experience and not knowing the background of what I personally had been through over a decade earlier surely didn't help them understand my perspective or the complete reasons for what had evolved. That's the risk we take when we keep our children in the dark for what we (at the time) considered to be for their own good. When you keep the children in the dark you might be protecting them in the short-term but in the long run they will never be able to fully grasp the truth because it's not what they grew up with and were conditioned with through a good chunk of their lives.

I've met many divorcees who didn't wait for their children to grow older before terminating their marriage. That route comes with its own set of challenges (visitation schedules, psychological impacts, the introduction of a second home, being a single parent, etc....). There is no way to judge which way (waiting or not waiting) is the better of the two because each one comes with equally damaging consequences. All I can say is that divorce sucks for children no matter how or when it occurs. My circumstance was even more dramatic than usual, and I do not blame my children if a good chunk of their childhood memories consisted of their father being a stern, irritable and explosive man. No, it's not who I am but yes it surely had to be a portion of what they viewed. I can spend the next two decades in therapy sessions trying to figure out how to right those wrongs.

If I were to sit here and make excuses, I would blame society for putting the pressures of success on our shoulders. We are all pushed into this rat race where it becomes the norm and acceptable to live up to one's means instead of being frugal and living for tomorrow. The wise elders in Brooklyn failed to teach me the proper lessons on what to do with money because they themselves really didn't have much. I made the same financial mistakes that most Americans continue to make as I type these words and that is:

1. that I failed to put away money for future (for that "rainy day")
2. that I lived beyond my means.

I may have had the Jaguar, the SUV, the boat, the wave runners and the horse trailer in the driveway but more important I should have had $70k to $80k stashed away in my savings account for just in case.

Those words "just in case" can mean a thousand different things for any one of us.

"Just in case you lose your job."

"Just in case you get sick."

"Just in case something happens to the house."

"Just in case the economy takes a turn for the worst."

"Just in case we experience a worldwide pandemic."

Or in my scenario, "Just in case I get into a car accident that causes me to lose my mojo and my ability to earn a decent income." That just in case fund is all I really needed to have bailed myself out of that financial jam and to most likely have avoided a long list of consequences that ensued. I screwed up and I screwed up bigtime. If I should be fortunate enough someday to be looked upon as a wise elder then surely I will incorporate into my teachings a long list of reasons why it's so darn important to live within one's means and to save, save, save money for the future. Those words are repeated by many but practiced by so few of us.

I really have no excuse for not being prepared. So much for the Boy Scout Motto.

Perhaps the optimist in me simply had me always preparing for success and never preparing for failure. All this makes me wonder if the added eliminate of surprise contributed to my turmoil.

Getting caught off-guard is surely an understatement.

I was blindsided by my own poor planning. I was the creator of my own demise. The devil himself may have been the operator of that truck but all he really did was set me off on a course that I had already plotted without realizing it. He really didn't have to do much other than give me a simple nudge in the wrong direction. It's as if he knew that I had no backup plan to cover any of the just in case scenarios.

What a tricky little devil he is. Then again, isn't that how the devil always works? Reminds me much like the way God works (if you believe in God). Both the devil and God just sit back and watch as we create and destroy. They observe us as we help and hurt, cry and laugh, and as we stand and fall. All they ever really do is give us a nudge here and there in one direction or the other and we, the creators of our own destiny, do all the rest. The devil is said to be the nemesis of good people. I disagree. It's clear to me that WE are our OWN nemesis.

The devil made me do it and this is all the work of the devil are both fallacies.

All this makes even more sense why I was so hard on myself when my life continued to spiral out of control. I was surely self-loathing because deep down inside I knew that what I perceived as misfortune caused by the devil was the inevitable that was self-inflicted. Makes one wonder about and rethink the concept of being the master of one's own destiny. Up until this point I only ever thought about it in the positive:

"Her hard work earned her the promotion."
"Their dedication toward their goals yielded fantastic results ahead of schedule."

I never once thought about the negative effects of one's actions and how they contribute toward the future. Once again, I discover yet another disadvantage of being the ultimate optimist. I'm also beginning to discover that a realist would never make such an oversight. This, in turn, makes me wonder:

Do realists have dreams/goals/aspirations?

It's said that realists cannot have romantic ideals and that they are like pragmatists. That's all great but I still don't understand how anyone can exist and succeed without having dreams and setting goals toward obtaining them. It's like taking the thunder out of a good summer storm (because it's the rumble of thunder that really defines a summer storm as being significant). Speaking of thunder and rumbling I look back now at my own ranting and raving and I wonder where the heck all that energy came from. In the height of my own storm, I could really dish it out. Perhaps it was my unsettled frustrations that fueled my fury. Whatever the root of it was, I can tell you that it supplied enough fuel to sustain a frenzy that outlasted any rage I've ever experienced (and probably ever will experience).

Uncontrollable rage often makes headlines in the media. I'm not sure why society is so fascinated by a huge riot, act of war or domestic violence incident. Why we are obsessed with turmoil is beyond me. Why we are obsessed when others are bullied is truly disturbing to me. Perhaps it makes us feel like our lives are little bit better than what we thought they were. It could be that at-least-I'm-not-that-bad mentality. The truth is though that any level of badness is too much. We need to live our lives in harmony. I've already mentioned the importance of balance a few times (and I'll surely mention it again). When balance exists, harmony is the sound it makes. To live one's life in harmony is to dance to the song of near perfect balance. I wish it was as easy to achieve as it sounds. Truth of the matter is that we are always in a constant struggle to keep everything in our world around us as well as everything inside us (both physically, emotionally and spiritually) in balance. It's a struggle that I'm not sure anyone can ever really truly perfect.

Back to the rage... With every outburst of rage comes a cool-down period of remorse, regret and shame. Words cannot be unspoken and unfortunate for us, in our times of rage we can say some harsh, nasty words (many of which we probably don't truly mean or feel). You cannot undo any of those words once we unleash them. When I was a child, I tended to act quicker than my mind could process. Come to think of it, I've been that same way even into adulthood. My father recognized this attribute about me, and he would often drill these words into my head:

"Think before you do."

He was so adamant about instilling this ideology into my life that he even signed my sixth-grade yearbook with those words in bold letters. If only I would have been a better listener. Let me rephrase that; if only I'd been a better follower. Surely, I heard his instructions loud and clear. Surely, I knew I tended to still act and speak impulsively. My problem was with the execution of his advice. I simply could not think my words or actions through before saying or doing them. It's a curse or flaw (or whatever you want to call it) that I've carried with me my entire life. This flaw of mine only compounded my problems. You see, it was bad enough that I carried around with me all that rage about the building debt with no foreseeable solution in sight. But I also carried around with me all that frustration for not being able to do my job the way that I knew I could do it. One of the most horrible feelings for an overachiever is to be nonproductive and to be aware of one's lack of productivity. It eats at you like a leech gnawing on your skin sucking the life out of you.

Add to all this my inability to control the words that come out of my mouth and you have the perfect recipe for the creation of a madman. My parents, siblings and ex-girlfriend were in the firing line when I lost my vision. My children, friends, physicians and ex-wife were in the firing line when I lost my mojo. During the aftermath of both, my self-esteem was in the firing line for knowing that I lashed-out and took my sorrows out on those who were closest to me.

Why we do this is beyond my comprehension. Perhaps it's because we are self-destructive. Or perhaps it's because we aim for the easiest targets. Whatever the reason… whatever the cause… let it be known that the aftermath is the worst part. The rage itself is a powerplay. We don't feel bad while we are doing it. If anything, we feel a satisfying release to let out some of the steam that's been building up inside us.

Keep in mind, that every argument has three sides, your side, their side and the right side (which usually lies somewhere in between). So not to say that I was anywhere close to being justified for saying any of the mean or strict words I've said during these rages, one can still argue that I wasn't always 100% in the wrong. It's the way I approached the problem/conflict that was 100% entirely the wrong way. In other words, the message or intent might have been somewhat justified or rooted in something wholesome and of real concern. I just ruined the delivery of the message by turning to anger instead of to reason.

The aftermath hurt. It was completely frustrating to know that I had something that was important to me to communicate but instead I ruined the communication by being argumentative and confrontational. Even worse was the feeling when I did it toward my children. I always considered one of my greatest successes in my lifetime to be the raising of my children. But at that moment… during the aftermath of one of my unwarranted rages, I felt like a failure as a parent. Likewise, I always patted myself on the back for being a dependable, trustworthy and accommodating spouse. I would often receive compliments from women on how lucky my ex-wife was that I did all the cooking and a good part of the laundry and cleaning around the house in addition to almost all the mentoring for the children. But in the aftermath of me being an unreasonable prick to my ex-wife and not knowing how to properly and effectively communicate with her, in my mind I was reduced to nothing more than a less-than-average spouse who had just as many moments of glory as I did moments of shame.

The truth is, there is no handbook on how to be a good father or how to be a good spouse. The wise elders of Brooklyn taught me a thing or two about these subjects but for some reason during the years that followed my car accident I was having a serious problem retrieving the memories of many of those ever-so-important lessons. That's when I started to realize that part of losing my mojo involved losing the instincts that I had honed over the years that were rooted in the knowledge that the elders from Brooklyn passed on to me. It was the strangest feeling to be aware that I was unaware of that which had become second nature to me. Head injuries can be tricky like that (and that is why they are often difficult to diagnose).

If I had clear-cut amnesia whereas I couldn't remember my name or what city I was born in or how to do multiplication, most neurologists or even family practitioners would have no problem putting a diagnosis in writing. But when a patient tells a doctor, "Hey doc, I can't remember my instincts." Well most physicians wouldn't know what to do with that information. Most of the time this would surely leave the patient untreated. In my case it left me with the inability to retrieve what absolutely amounted to some of the most valuable knowledge I had accumulated over my lifetime. Without knowing it, my memories were missing much of which I would normally regard as common sense.

This clearly was the why behind the reason I lost my mojo. Imagine missing all of the known existence as well as the ammunition that defended it and the fuel that kept it all going. Society often doesn't give enough credit to the value of knowledge. Yes, we use sayings such as Brains over Brawn. But do we really mean it?

Do we really believe that mental acuity can beat great physical strength?

Once upon a time I was certain that the answer to that question was yes. Once upon a time I had all my ducks in order too. All this discovering that chunks of memory and common sense were missing led to a revelation in my head:

I realized that for a third time in my life I had gone blind; only this time it wasn't my eyes that could not see.

This time it was my mental acuity that had lost its vision. This new discovery sent me even further spiraling downward into the darkness of the abyss. It was a discovery that I simply could not stomach. I doubt even my persona at 100% capacity would have been prepared to process and deal with this magnitude of a setback. Hitting me with it at that point in time was like kicking me in the groin after I was already down on the ground.

When we are growing up we often make mistakes, take some unnecessary risks and say lots of foolish things that we learn to regret. These missteps are all part of life and as we continue to learn from those experiences we evolve into wiser, more informed and more conditioned people. The longer we live the more of this wisdom we accumulate. Now imagine for a moment that you lost all ability to retrieve those lessons that life taught you. Add to that the loss of the lessons and knowledge that you accumulated from reading books, all of the tidbits of advice that you received from the lectures from your parents, school-teachers, religious leaders, coaches and scout leaders as well as all the knowledge you've ever accumulated from listening to the experiences of your peers and your siblings. We are talking about several lifetimes of knowledge that was all crammed inside of your memory banks and now it is instantly irretrievable.

Complete and total devastation. This is the only way I would and could describe what it felt like to discover that my memory banks were unreadable. My brain was like a computer that couldn't retrieve and decipher any of the most important files stored within. However, unlike a computer, I had no reboot or reset button to press to attempt to correct the situation. There was no software I could download to scan for any remaining scattered pieces of information. I was hopelessly the recipient of what felt like the cruelest of punishments. The discovery angered me beyond any line I had ever crossed in my lifetime. It transformed me from being that irritable, asshole with the explosive temper to being something far worse for my existence to accept. It turned me into an always-bitter, hopeless PESSIMIST.

Chapter 12

The only other time in my life when I came close to transforming into a pessimist was immediately after my body rejected my first cornea transplant setting me back into a world of blindness. That tiny piece of donated tissue was my lifeline and I ruined it by not following Doctor Buxton's protocol. I smoked. I drank. I stayed out late. I allowed my body to feel worn down and out of steam. I didn't eat healthy nor did I get enough sleep. Sometimes I would skip a dose of my anti-rejection eye drops either because I would be too lazy to put them in or I would simply forget. It's no wonder my body rejected the cornea as quickly as it did.

At the time of my first surgery it was declared that the average lifespan of a transplanted cornea was projected to be between ten and fifteen years. Later studies over the decades concluded that it's closer to seventeen years. My first one lasted less than six months and it wasn't because the transplanted tissue died. I lost that first transplanted cornea solely due to my immune system attacking and killing it. Irony once again entered my life. This time it was the fact that my own immune system was being the bully destroying my new hope for regaining my vision. When my eye fogged-over from all the white blood cells filling up the cornea I knew EXACTLY what I had done. I took that spark... that hope for a life of new sight and I destroyed it. I was very aware of the fault being 100% mine. I took ownership of it. I accepted it. That revelation could've and should've launched me into a lifetime of pessimistic thoughts or at the very least a lifetime of low self-esteem.

Dr. Buxton proved to be my saving grace. Initially he was utterly disappointed. However even though there was less than a five percent chance that he could be victorious battling my immune system he gave it a go when he increased my meds for a week to see if they could have any positive effect. He tried. He really did try. And a week later when he discovered that his regime of medication had lost that battle with my immune system, he still did not give up hope. I'll never forget the sensation of him grabbing my hand with his as he spoke to me because his hand felt cold and smooth exactly like a medical instrument (which was ironic because in many ways his hands were medical instruments).

Dr Buxton held my hand with his as he explained to me how he had a plan to deal with my immune system using a combination of trickery and modern science. But first he explained to me how under normal circumstances there ordinarily would not have been much hope for someone with such a severe transplant rejection. My immune system was simply too over-powering. Then he forewarned me that even if his plan worked for my now-rejected right cornea I was going to have to wait another decade for my immune system to calm down as I grew older before any attempt could be made to perform a cornea transplant on my left eye. This meant that the best-case scenario was that I would regain vision in just one of my eyes and that I would have to wait ten years to try regaining the vision in my other eye. Dr. Buxton then informed me that it was my lucky day. His statement felt like an extremely ironic and even cruel thing to say to me considering the circumstances. However, little did I know that Dr. Buxton had just received funding to find patients to participate in a clinical study and I was a prime candidate. The study was aimed at taking the normally ingested anti-rejection medication, Cyclosporine-A and turning it into a topical eye drop. He explained to me that if successful, there would be two huge benefits to the patient.

The first being that the entire immune system throughout the body would not have to be suppressed (as is the effects of the ingested version of the medication). That benefit alone was clearly a huge plus for any transplant recipient.

The second huge benefit for the patient was the ability to specifically target just the cornea as the area where the drug would suppress the immune system in a dosage that would be much higher than what an ingested version of the medication could ever supply to the eye.

Now here was the catch (and where the trickery would come to play its part). For me to participate in the clinical trial I would need to undergo another cornea transplant in the same eye where the original cornea transplant was rejected. The problem with that was the fact that my eye was still the battleground for an all-out war that my immune system had declared on that first cornea transplant. There was no stopping my immune system and it's not like we could enter into a peace treaty with my white blood cells.

Dr. Buxton's answer to that dilemma was to leave the battle alone and let it continue. He explained that completely cutting out the rejected cornea and replacing it with a new donor's cornea would only expose that new cornea to the battle that the rejected one had already lost so quickly. This was due to the fact that I mentioned earlier how my body had grown an angry blood vessel at the base of the cornea from the sclera (white of the eye). That blood vessel would surely pump a healthy supply of white blood cells into any new foreign tissue that replaces the one under attack.

Trickery?

Yes.

Dr. Buxton had a plan to trick on my immune system. Instead of completely removing the rejected cornea he had a plan which involved leaving the lower portion of the rejected cornea in my eye and transplanting another cornea using a smaller diameter and placing it in my eye off-center away from the angry blood vessel. His thinking was that my immune system would continue to be preoccupied with that piece of the original cornea transplant that he left attached to my eye and since there are no blood vessels within the cornea itself he would be placing the newer cornea at a safe enough distance from that battleground.

Dr. Buxton's plan was ingenious, but it came with a lifetime of emotional baggage.

For starters I would have to sign my life away to be a lab rat, guinea pig or whatever you wanted to call someone who science was asking permission to experiment upon. There were no guarantees to be made. Cyclosporine-A was created to be an oral drug (not an eye drop). That turned out to be a bit of a scientific challenge because the drug was not water-soluble. It turned out that Cyclosporine-A was only oil-soluble. That meant the scientists had to find a suitable sterile oil-base that was also non-toxic to mix the drug with.

The solution?

Extra virgin olive oil!

Basically, I'd be administering drops of extra virgin olive oil infused with Cyclosporine-A into my eye.

Lab rat?

Yes, clearly, I had to agree to become one if I were to agree to participate in the clinical trial.

Next up on the emotional rollercoaster was the fact that I had to muster up the strength to go back on the transplant list once again as well as go through all of the steps of the recovery process including travelling back and forth to Manhattan again to deal with the removal of the dozens of sutures. I also had to deal with taping an eye shield to my head (I looked like a pirate) every night to protect the new cornea while I slept. Then there was going to be the constant worrying that my immune system would still discover the new cornea and reject it despite the trickery and topically administering the Cyclosporine-A solution.

Moreover was the guilt that the cost and inconvenience the medication carried with it. Health insurance and prescription plans don't cover experimental medications and this clinical trial did not cover the cost of the medication either. A one-month's supply cost $175 back in 1989 which is the equivalent of around $400 in 2021. Not a deal-breaker but when you consider that the average salary in New York in 1989 was only $20,000 you can understand better how $175/month was more like the equivalent of two car payments. And since this was an experimental

197

medication made specifically for the trial participants it was only going to be available at the New York Eye and Ear Infirmary where they would be infusing the extra virgin olive oil with the drug. That meant additional monthly trips into Manhattan whenever my regular visits with Dr. Buxton didn't coincide with obtaining a new month's supply of the eye drops.

On a final note, I had to also deal with the emotional baggage that came with having to keep a piece of the fogged-over rejected first cornea transplant attached to my eye for the rest of my life. It would be there for others to see (literally like an eye-sore).

All these thoughts were spinning through my head as I contemplated on whether to agree to Dr. Buxton's plan. The emotional baggage was topped-off with the fact that at that point I already had the DNA of another person permanently attached to my body and now I was going to have the DNA of a third person permanently attached. And if all went as planned and a decade later, I would have the cornea in my left eye transplanted that would translate into the DNA of yet a fourth person. Get the drift? Then there was the understanding that corneal transplants lasted only ten to fifteen years which meant eventually going back on the donation waiting list for each eye and going through the process all over again every ten to fifteen years of my life. If the proposition of participating in an experimental clinical trial didn't make me feel like a lab rat, then the thought that one day I'd be walking around with the DNA of half dozen or more other people surely made me feel like a lab freak. I had to stop and ask myself, what on Earth was I agreeing to become?

On the flip side of the coin was the clear and precise argument, what did I really have to lose? I was already legally blind. I already had one eye sliced and diced. I survived the crazy glue saga as if it never happened and this was going to be a controlled and highly monitored procedure. The aftercare especially was going to be crucial. Immediately following the first transplant I was scheduled to see Dr. Buxton every seven to ten days This time around it was going to be every four to five days. The clinical trial was important to him which meant the survival of my second cornea transplant was on the top of his list of priorities. Dr. Buxton was leaving no wiggle room for failure. He even explained to me how in his absence I would be seen by his son, Dr. Douglas Buxton. This was personal to him and it was his personal interest that convinced me that I was making the right decision to agree to the clinical trial as well as his plan to leave a piece of the rejected cornea in my eye.

What helped convince me even more was a brief encounter with one of his other patients named Michelle in his waiting room. I couldn't see her, nor could she see me because we were both legally blind. I was later told by my mother that Michelle had what appeared to be burns all over her face and arms. I remember her name clearly after all of these years because in making small talk, I asked whether she spelled her name with one letter 'L' or two (because my mom named one of my sisters Michele with one 'L.') I recall Michelle explaining to me how she had just learned that she is not a candidate for a cornea transplant in either of her eyes due to her condition. It turned out that she had an extremely rare condition known as Stevens-Johnson Syndrome.

Want to talk about bad luck?

How about a medical condition that causes an ordinary medication to create a painful rash on your skin, eyes, even up your nose and within your genitals. That rash then blisters like a second degree burn until the skin dies and sheds. For Michelle it was believed to have been triggered by a single dose of ordinary Penicillin. The rash left behind are scars that never disappear.

Michelle could never undergo cornea transplants because of the scars on her eyes. My conversation with her was brief but meaningful in so many ways. It made me once again have the realization that no matter how bad you think you have it in life there is always someone else out there who is worse off than you. Our conversation also reminded me how fortunate I was to be presented with the opportunity for not just a do-over but one that involved cutting-edge pharmaceuticals and a cutting-edge strategy.

Signing that clinical trial agreement might have made me into a certified lab-rat but at least I was Dr. Buxton's lab rat and I had full faith that he would make sure that this lab rat's story was as successful one. So on to the donation waiting list my name once again was added.

When I look back on that period, I can't help but to think that Dr. Buxton saved me in more ways than one. For obvious reasons he put me back on the road toward regaining my vision. However just as equally as important, he saved me from crossing over to the dark side and becoming a pessimist.

I was almost there.

The rejection of my cornea and the likelihood that I was never going to receive another cornea in that eye was a real threat. It was real enough to have put me over that edge and lose all hope that positive things do indeed occur and that you simply must continue to put out positive energy into this world in order to receive some of it back.

A month later and my second cornea transplant was stitched into my eye. During the first transplant I didn't ask many questions because part of me didn't want to know the answers. The second time around I was full of questions about the procedure. I learned that in order to create a perfect sized transplanted tissue from the donated cornea a device that looks like a tiny little cookie-cutter is used. First, it's used on the donated cornea to cut a perfectly round piece. Then the recipient's eye is drained of the interior fluid and the cookie-cutter device is used to cut away the same size diameter from the recipient's eye (with precision, of course!). Next the donated cornea is placed over the void that was left behind by the cookie-cutter device and it's held in place by a few dozen sutures.

Apparently, the stitching is the art form. That's where the surgeon earns his keep. Stitch too tight in some locations and the new cornea will stretch or even tear. Stitch too loosely and the new cornea might develop wrinkles that will distort the vision or even make it near impossible to fit the new cornea with a gas permeable contact lens. Keep in mind the sutures themselves are tiny as hell.

When you wake up from the surgery the eye is covered by a metal shield to prevent the patient from accidentally injuring the new cornea or worse yet, popping a stitch. I don't have any recollection of waking up from my first surgery. It was in the late afternoon/early evening and for all I know I could've slept through recovery. However, I have perfect memories of waking up after my second surgery. It was a very sunny day. The recovery room was so bright from the sunshine that I immediately could focus upon the gauze that lined the inside of the medal shield. It had a sort of tic-tac-toe pattern to it. The fact that I was focusing on anything brought a smile to my face. No more foggy vision. The new cornea was in its new home.

Without me even asking, a nurse working the recovery unit informed me that she read my chart and learned that the donor was an eighteen-year-old boy who was struck and killed by a drunk driver. I sometimes wonder if these background stories I am told about the donors are true or perhaps they just tell random made-up stories to add extra meaning to the transplant recipient's mind in hopes that he or she will safeguard their new gift knowing that someone had to die in order for them to receive it. I'd like to think that the background stories are indeed true and will hold on to them as if they are. With that being said, I had more than just a moment where I felt bad for the teenager whose family was kind enough to donate his corneas (and probably some of his organs too).

The removal of the shield is the first of two exciting moments that follow a cornea transplant. It's exciting because there is always a drastic improvement in vision. For a very small elite few, that translates into vision that doesn't even need corrective contact lenses or eyeglasses. I've never been one of them. For the bulk of us, improvement in vision means no longer seeing eighteen halos when you look outside at the streetlights at night. Instead now there are only two or three (I kid you not). It also means being able to squint my way around a room and even being able to read something that is held a few inches away from my face. These might sound barbaric, but they are indeed drastic improvements. But the removal of the shield is only the teaser.

The most exciting moment occurs six to twelve months after the surgery when a gas permeable contact lens is placed on the cornea for the very first time. I've never taken a hit of heroin (nor do I ever plan to). From what I've read it's so intense that one hit is all it takes to be addicted for life. Well I can imagine what that intense hit feels like because the sensation of going from being legally blind to obtaining 20/20 vision within a split second is surreal. It's pure euphoria like no other sensation that I've ever experienced. Weeks upon weeks of having sutures removed mixed with daily doses of Cyclosporine-A infused extra virgin olive oil drops in my eyes as well as countless eye exams all led up to that very moment and there are no words to truly describe how incredible it feels for the optic nerve to pass on meaningful clear vision from the retina to the visual cortex within the occipital lobe of the brain. It's a mad rush that's for sure.

Successful cornea transplantation is measured in four ways.

The first is obviously controlling the immune system and keeping it at bay. The second is the orchestrated removal of the sutures (for the same reasons why suture placement is crucial so is suture removal at the right time spaced apart at the right distance to avoid pulling or twisting of the cornea).

The third is the control of intraocular pressure (pressure of the fluid within the eye being too high is the second leading cause of lost transplants and unfortunately the anti-rejection steroid drops often have a side effect of increasing interocular pressure).

And naturally the fourth (and to the patient the hands-down most important) measure of success is the vision that is obtained using corrective lenses.

Regaining lost vision meant seeing objects, people and places with clarity for the first time in a very long time. Even the simplest of objects (such as cracks in a sidewalk or leaves on a tree) can be an intriguing sight when visualized for the first time in many years. It was great to actually be able to watch a movie instead of just listening to it. It was incredible to see the faces of my family and friends once again. But out of everything I got to experience again for the first time I think the most intriguing was looking at myself in the mirror for the first time in a very long time. Talk about a head-rush. I thought about how I looked older than I felt. Then my vision focused upon the clouded spot beneath my right cornea where the rejection battle is still taking place to this very day with the section of the first cornea transplant that Dr. Buxton purposely left in my eye. It is a constant reminder of my ordeal and how grateful I should be that I can obtain any sort of useful vision out of either of my eyes. The struggle is real, and I have the battle wounds to prove it.

I was on my best behavior during the months and years that followed that second surgery.

I followed Dr. Buxton's directions precisely. I never missed an appointment and rarely, if ever missed a single dose of my medication. Eventually the clinical trial ended, and I was placed on the traditional immune suppressing steroid drops. I had a few close calls throughout the years with my right cornea where my intraocular pressure was too high. Luckily it was brought under control using Glaucoma medication. Other than a few scary bouts with conjunctivitis (pink eye), that eighteen-year old's cornea has been holding up pretty darn strong over the years as it has flown way past the average seventeen-year life expectancy. That second surgery was in 1989 which puts the age of the right cornea transplant at over THIRTY years old and holding on strong!

And as for my left eye, just as Dr. Buxton (may he now rest in peace) promised, I was able to receive a cornea transplant in 1999. With the help of new high-tech sclera lenses (they sit on the white of the eyes instead of on the corneas and they ride on a cushion of fluid between the lenses and the corneas) I am able to obtain 20-20 vision despite the fact that I am still legally blind in both of my eyes without the assistance of the lenses. It's been over twenty years since the cornea transplant in my left eye. Not yet as impressive as my right eye but still pretty darn good I'd say.

Oh boy did things change ten years later when I received the transplant in my left eye.

Instead of a three to five day inpatient hospital stay after undergoing general anesthesia (as I did during the 1989 procedures) the 1999 surgery was performed on an outpatient basis while I was awake and under what they called a twilight anesthesia.

You want to talk about a freaky experience?

Imagine seeing that cookie-cutter device coming straight at your eye while your head is clamped to the table and feeling the pressure as it cuts out the circular piece of your cornea. I swear it felt like something out of a horror movie. Recovery was basically the same although sutures are removed more quickly and unless there are complications most patients are fitted with a contact lens at around six to eight months post-surgery. Unlike the first two transplants, I was never informed what the age or cause of death was of the donor. Other than that, and a few advances in how they match donor tissue to the recipient, most of the procedure is the same using sutures and immune suppressant steroid drops.

It may be over thirty years since I regained my vision but I still to this day consider myself the luckiest man alive. I'll never take anything in this world for granted again. Losing one's vision may possibly be one of the top ten worse things in the world that could ever happen to a person (with death obviously being number one) yet if you ever met me and I didn't share my experience with you, I can say with 100% certainty that you would never be able to guess that I've lived through such an ordeal. I will say that it's taught me to pursue my dreams TODAY because there may never be a tomorrow or tomorrow may never be what you expected it to be like.

I also learned that at our darkest hour when there seems like no hope exists, we all have a fighting chance to encounter our very own 444 to lift us out of the abyss.

Always hold your head up high and be proud of your accomplishments just as this runt of the litter is proud of his. Sometimes things go as planned but more often than not, they deviate from the paths that we choose and head off in entirely different directions. Sometimes we can fight our way back on to the paths that we desire but other times we must go with the flow and put our faith in the hands of a Dr. Buxton. Not every plan is going to be ideal so often we must simply go with the one that makes the most logical sense.

I can't help but to mention Michelle once again. I think of her courage fighting a battle that cannot be won and yet she still had this calmness in her voice as if she knew that everything was going to be okay for her. It's kind of like the way I felt when I poured super glue into my eye. It clearly appeared to be a situation where I was going to lose my entire eye yet there was this calmness that took over and assured me that everything was going to be alright. Michelle had that tone in her voice. I also can't help but to once again mention how her suffering served a purpose by reminding me and countless others that no matter how bad our situations may seem there is always someone else less fortunate than we are. The only problem with that is the fact that not everyone who is less fortunate than us is able to be saved in time (or in many cases, capable of being saved).

I'm speaking directly about those who find that free-fall into the abyss and the fear of impact at the bottom too frightening to tolerate another day. Suicide is a real threat to more people in this world than many of us realize because for the most part by the time those who are at high risk of pulling that trigger reach the point of almost no return they are usually so silent about it that their pain and struggle often go unnoticed until it's simply too late. Victims of bullying often find themselves without any hope or coping mechanisms. Bullying to this very day continues to be a major threat to children of all age groups but especially adolescents and young adults. This age group also must deal with the added stress of major life changes as they begin to assume more adult roles and responsibility.

Adolescents and young adults can often feel isolated by relationships-gone-wrong. Also, their tendencies to experiment with drugs and alcohol adds a whole another dimension to the equation. Part of it is because the drugs and alcohol distort ones' perception of reality which opens the door for suicidal thoughts to become significantly amplified. The other reason is simply because drugs and alcohol make it easier to commit suicide either by becoming the lethal dosage itself or by lowering self-consciousness so much that otherwise terrifying acts become as spontaneous as tying one's shoes.

I dated a girl for many years who eventually went on to take her own life in her early twenties. I started dating her shortly after regaining my vision and our relationship lasted just shy of four years. The girl I knew showed very little signs of ever being capable of committing suicide. She seemed to love life. The only dark shadow of her past that possibly could have suggested that she would one day find herself at a train station waiting to leap in front of the next on-coming train was a story from her youth about her best friend who took her own life at a tender young age of fourteen.

Back in the 1980s, Post Traumatic Stress Disorder (PTSD) was only something that war veterans and kidnapping victims were regarded to experience. Nobody ever imagined that a firefighter could be prone to PTSD nor could anyone envision that a child who lived through her best friend's successful suicide attempt experienced enough distraught to plant that PTSD seed that, if left untreated can grow into a self-destructive monster. Unfortunate for me (and it's something that I must live with for the rest of my life) the trigger that may have ignited that time bomb inside of her that was waiting to explode was our break-up. It didn't go very smoothly and to make matters even worse for her to handle I met and was engaged to my first wife within a year or so after the break-up.

If there is such a thing as a trigger that can set off a suicide waiting to happen then surely it was the combination of our break-up along with the successful suicide of her closest cousin (and literally her new best friend) all within a short period of time. So now we have what anyone would consider to be a normally healthy and ordinary young woman who experienced the tragedies of losing her childhood best friend along with her favorite beloved cousin to suicide and throw in there the loneliness and feeling of rejection from our break-up combined with the fact that my new engagement meant that there was little-to-no hope of us ever getting back together and you have all of the ingredients for the perfect storm to bring on that night at the train station.

What sucks even more for me and has me convinced that her suicide was some sort of message to me was the shocking fact that she took her life on the evening of what would have been our anniversary together. There are three hundred and sixty-five days in the year. There is no way that anyone will ever convince me that she did not chose that exact date in the middle of October on purpose knowing that someday I would see the date and become aware just as no one will ever convince me that she didn't purposely choose the exact train that her father would commute home from work on.

Her final resting place is in the same cemetery as two of my grandparents as well as my brother-in-law. I can't help myself from time to time to pay a visit to her grave and just stare at that date on her tombstone. I know there is nothing I could have done to prevent it simply because as I mentioned before by the time someone in her shoes approaches that point of no return, they are usually so silent and secretive about what they are going through that not another living soul can possibly have awareness of the tragedy that is about to take place. I was later told that on that very same day she received professional therapy. So even a trained therapist may not have the eye to spot the signs of a suicide waiting to happen.

The lesson here is not to make any assumptions. If you know of someone who has been through turmoil or who seems to have retreated into the depths of their own mind don't hesitate to reach out and offer a shoulder to lean on. Sometimes all it takes is an ounce of goodwill to spring someone out of their misery enough to realize that suicide isn't their only option. Unfortunately, the 444 vision through a pinhole doesn't always come in time for everyone so therefore don't hesitate to be someone's 444.

Chapter 13

I'm a firm believer in Karma...
you get what you give, good or bad.
                                        –Sandra Bullock.

I write this to you as I sit on the porch of Sandra Bullock's beach house on Tybee Island just outside of Savannah Georgia. I found the quote from Sandra about Karma on the internet. This house is exactly not what you would expect of a multi-millionaire mega-star (and that's what makes it so awesome). It's got a Southern old-world charm that screams SIMPLICITY.

The furniture is quaint. The rooms are small and homely. The floors creak and so does the plumbing. If this house was ever remodeled in the past, you'd have to be an expert in architecture to prove it. In the upstairs bathroom there is a small sign posted above the bathtub instructing guests on the precautions they should take to prevent the bath water from leaking through the floor and out the ceiling above the dining room below. If it weren't for the occasional flat panel televisions with their $400 rechargeable universal remotes or the world-class gourmet kitchen you'd almost be able to pretend as if you took a journey back in time to an era of more simplicity.

There is no doubt that Sandra chose this romantic hideaway as a place for her and the children to escape from the big city lights and the hustle/bustle of the Hollywood scene. While exploring the three bedrooms upstairs I came across a children's room with bunk beds. They reminded me of the simplest time in my life when my two daughters shared a room with bunk beds. My favorite thing in the world to do at that time was to tell them adlib bedtime stories with each of them being the main characters of the stories. I do believe by their reactions (and their constant requests for more stories to be told) that at that time in their lives those adlib stories were the most favorite thing in their lives too.

Reminiscing about this makes me both joyous and saddened at the same time. I am so appreciative to have created those precious moments with them but at the same time I passionately miss them. That's the thing about raising children. Time flies so quickly. One moment you are in the thick of it all and the next moment it's nothing more than a memory of one big blur of diapers, car seats and bedtime stories. I guess the same can be said for our own childhoods. One moment we are runts of the litter roaming the streets with our bicycles and with what feels like a blink of an eye we find ourselves all grown up with children of our own.

When we are children, we tend to see the world more clearly. The lessons of life are more apparent and our ability to decipher what is important and what is irrelevant is spot-on. One of the first lessons in life that we learn from our experiences is that balance is important. Mother nature doesn't fair well when there is imbalance. Neither does our health or our lives. I was fortunate enough to learn this from the old timers from Brooklyn along with all the other pieces of wisdom they bestowed on me. The problem with transforming into adulthood is that we get so consumed with adulting that we often forget 90% of the lessons we learn when we are children.

Unfortunately, many of us forget the second lesson in life that we often learn and that is the one Sandra Bullock is referring to regarding Karma. Become a believer that the world is full of energy. Each of us put out our own energy into the world. Put out positive energy and positive energy will find its way back to you in some other form. But put out negative energy and eventually you will be the recipient of something that impacts you negatively as well. The rules of karma follow the rules of balance and there simply is no cheating them or avoiding the consequences of our actions. In the end, Karma always ultimately dictates your faith. Be a good person even during times when nobody else is being good to you. Karma will return your positive energy to you.

When I was at wit's end without a shred of patience or mental stamina left after losing my mojo I became a very bitter person. Being so bitter I put out constant negative energy only to have karma send it back my way. This is a vicious cycle that so many people find themselves caught in. It's vicious because the negative karma coming back at you makes you an even bitter person than what you started out to be. At this point I had lost count of how many times I've been shoved back into a freefall through the darkness. When you are a teenager without anyone in the world depending on you it's easier to cover up what you are going through emotionally.

When you are an adult, a father, a husband, a company representative, and a contributing member of society it isn't so easy to bury your head in the sand and not have anyone around you take notice. I was spiraling out of control with the weight of the world on my shoulders. Bedtime stories ceased. Family vacations and weekend getaways became nothing more than distant memories. I couldn't even remember when the last time was that I had a friendly conversation with another human being. I was approaching that point where the pain from the freefall into darkness was almost unbearable and just as I was arriving there a gift from the past saved my life.

Yes, I received a gift from the past but not the kind of gift that you would ever imagine. It started with a circuit breaker tripping. I can't remember what exactly caused the breaker to trip. Perhaps it was overloaded or perhaps it was simply an ounce of positive energy that I still had put out there into the universe a long time ago making its way back to me. Whatever caused that circuit breaker to trip literally saved my life because when I was in the garage resetting it, I noticed a cardboard box on the top of a shelf. The box looked vaguely familiar to me, but I couldn't pinpoint exactly what it was. When I blew off the dust and opened the cover to my surprise, I found that it contained a stack of over 300 handwritten pages of notes, poems and quoted lyrics. Written on the cover page were the words:

The Philosophy

Written on the first page within was a note addressed simply:

"To You..."

When I read the note, I immediately had goosebumps up and down my arms. What I had found was nothing short of a miracle. It was literally a handbook about life written by me from age 12 to age 18. Preserved within the pages were all the words of wisdom handed down to me throughout those years by the old timers in Brooklyn along with insights and revelations or "pieces of thought" as I called them.

How ironic was it that as a child I named the tidbits of common sense and learned knowledge "pieces of thought"?

Page after page contained golden nuggets... what felt like a lifetime of wisdom was all condensed within those 300 pages. On one page were the words:

My philosophy of life...
Live in the present.
Forget the bad past.
Don't worry about the future.
And never, ever, let anyone or anything phase you.

Throughout the pages were what amounted to be a guide on how to live a virtuous life. It covered multiple topics from relationships to karma, to the importance of balance and so on. The most relevant section I found for me at that time was pages upon pages labelled "How It's Done." That section was literally a handbook on how to be successful in business and in life.

Miraculously in that dusty old cardboard box on the shelf in the garage I found my mojo. The more I read **The**

Philosophy, the more it filled in the blanks in my mind. Everything that was lost... everything that was forgotten after my car accident was put back in place in my mind like putting together a jigsaw puzzle that had missing pieces. Everything fit perfectly in place. And just like that... like flipping a circuit breaker I was back.

The very first read through **The Philosophy** rivaled the intense euphoria of the very first time I placed a gas permeable contact lens on my new cornea. I could see again for the very first time in a very long time! Once again it was like an imaginary hit of a fantastic magical drug. I was instantly high on life again and it felt so incredibly great to feel all the new connections being made within my brain and most especially feeling as though my Neocortex had come back to life.

No more depression. No more irritability. No more fogginess. The teenage me came to my rescue. I began to kick ass at work again. Every aspect of my life improved. I got my life back together and then went on to meet and fall in love with my new wife with whom I started a fresh new life. Even to this day I find myself constantly referring to that cardboard box for guidance. It's become apparent to me that children possess a much clearer insight and are much more in-tune with the world than any adult could ever be. Maybe it's because they haven't yet been bogged-down and overwhelmed with all that life challenges us with or perhaps it's their innocence and purity that allows them to focus better. Whatever the reason is, surely, I am convinced now that the teenage version of me was far wiser than I ever gave him credit for being.

I will never claim to have all the answers to the questions that life presents to us.

However, what I didn't realize (up until that point) was that I lost my mojo because I lost the answers to a good percentage of the questions that I learned the answers to when I was a child. Written on those pages by the younger version of me were those lost answers. Years upon years of knowledge was literally shocked out of my Neocortex upon that head-on collision with the truck. Now it was all there in black-and-white for me to read, absorb and relearn. A lifetime of knowledge written by me and preserved in that dusty box. I couldn't help but to think that all that work to put all that knowledge in writing on those hundreds upon hundreds of pages was all intended for this precise moment in my life when I needed to read it the most. Within the pages of **The Philosophy** I make constant references to song lyrics. I never realized how persuasive and significant song lyrics could be. The first few times that I read through those pages it was a sort of head trip for me because it felt as though I was reading the work of a favorite author. It did not feel as though I was reading my own words. Even to this day I will read passages and reread them as if they are foreign to me. It's an astonishing experience to find your own words educational as well as entertaining. It makes me wonder if this sensation is a result of my head injury or do authors often read some of their earlier writings with a fresh set of eyes and find their own work to be a revelation?

I think the most difficult part of my road to recovery was picking up the broken pieces and attempting to figure out which ones can be put back together and which could not. Mounds of credit card debt just don't pay themselves off overnight and relationships aren't always salvageable. **The Philosophy** doesn't contain the answers to every problem that needed solving but it certainly set the tone and put me back on the right path. One thing I did learn on my own since that whole experience took place is that the first key to success and happiness is to be sure to surround yourself with a good set of people. I look back now on my car accident and the time when I lost my vision and I see so many parallels to my behavior and my reactions. Both were traumatic events in my life and both times I found myself falling out of control. Both times I lost my ability to see but just in different ways.

As tough as being the runt of the litter made me be, I still had my limits to what I was capable of handling. That's yet another life lesson: to know one's limits and know when it's safe and appropriate to attempt to exceed them. Once again it goes back to the lesson about how important it is to keep everything in life as balanced as possible. As far as relationships go, I was able to salvage some, but I also lost a few. One takeaway that I learned from it all is that it's important to stay as true and honest as possible. The people around you who really care about you will accept you for who you are not what you think you might need to pretend to be. They will accept you and your flaws but what they won't accept is dishonesty.

On the most intimate level I learned something about myself that isn't easy to admit. I discovered that I suffer from some sort of mental illness along with ADHD (Adult Attention-Deficit/Hyperactivity Disorder). Therapists and psychiatrists are very hesitant these days to place exact labels upon their patients so the most accurate description I could officially obtain so far is that I suffer from one or more "personality disorders." Apparently, there are ten different types of personality disorders but reading through the descriptions of each it's clear to me that mine leans more toward bipolar disorder along with ADHD than toward any of the others.

In many circles the words 'bipolar disorder' are associated with someone who is unstable and often flies off the deep end. I once had a personal discussion with one of the top producers in my industry. She openly told me how she was good at her job because she was bipolar, didn't need much sleep and often became obsessed with the 'high' of being successful. Her willingness to openly admit that she was bipolar opened my eyes and made me realize that ordinary as well as extraordinary people can suffer from bipolar and how it's nothing to be ashamed about. It reminded me of those who suffer from suicidal thoughts and how their secrecy often contributes toward their tragedy. It also was the first time that I was educated on the fact that bipolar and being an overachiever often go hand-in-hand together (who knew, right?).

Embracing a diagnosis and openly sharing it with others is in many ways equal to being victorious over the disease. Once again, if you surround yourself with good people, they will be supportive and help you cope with the challenges that you face no matter what they might be. I can tell you firsthand that the medications on the market today that are prescribed for personality disorders and ADHD are highly effective and many of them have very little side effects (if any at all). For someone like me who already feels like a bionic man managing my eyesight with a combination of prescriptions and high-tech lenses, popping a few pills to help control my mood swings and increase my ability to focus and remain on a stable course was clearly a no-brainer. Bipolar, ADHD and most other personality disorders are completely manageable in today's modern world. They are nothing to be ashamed of and certainly do not make any of us any less capable of achieving greatness in life.

The exact cause of bipolar disorder as well as ADHD are both unknown. Both are suspected to be caused by a combination of brain chemistry, genetics, environment and brain structure that contribute toward the cause. There is said to usually be some sort of trigger such as a traumatic event, a period of high stress or the death of a close loved-one that triggers the first few episodes of bipolar. For me it more than likely was triggered by going blind for the first time. All those times when my mom thought the steroid eye drops were making me irritable, she was on to something, but it wasn't the steroids that was the cause it was my undiagnosed personality disorder that was more than likely causing those mood swings. It's also very clear to me now that the trauma of that car accident triggered another event that lasted longer than it should have lasted had I been properly treated with medication.

Hey, you live and learn, right?

Another life lesson that I learned was that those of us who were bullied when we were younger are not alone. When we were younger it was often embarrassing to admit that we were bullied but now as an adult I am learning that being open and honest about it invites in others who can relate to the painful memories. There is comfort in sharing and there is comfort in numbers. So, if you were ever bullied and need relief from those torturous memories the best advice that I can give you is to communicate with those around you who you trust the most and you might be surprised to learn how many others were also bullied when they were younger and how those individuals and you can now relate to each other.

Last but most important is as we get older it's important for us to pass the torch on to the younger generations. One day it becomes our turn to be the old timers who instill our wisdom in the new generations. The world is such an imperfect place with so much turmoil especially among our society. Be a part of the solution and not a part of the problem. It all starts with inspiring our children and grandchildren and instilling the knowledge we possess into their minds. More important than anything else, inspire them to put their thoughts in writing, print them out and store them in a cardboard box in the garage because one never knows when they might someday lose their ability to see things the same way as they see them today.

"But I know this: I was blind, and now I can see!"
John 9:25

Printed in the USA
CPSIA information can be obtained
at www.ICGtesting.com
LVHW020245051023
760125LV00004B/331